Banking Union for Europe

Risks and Challenges

Centre for Economic Policy Research (CEPR)

Centre for Economic Policy Research
3rd Floor
77 Bastwick Street
London, EC1V 3PZ
UK

Tel: +44 (0)20 7183 8801
Fax: +4 (0)20 7183 8820
Email: cepr@cepr.org
Web: www.cepr.org

Published in association with the
London Publishing Partnership (www.londonpublishingpartnership.co.uk)

© Centre for Economic Policy Research, 2012

ISBN: 978-1-907142-57-4 (print edition)

Banking Union for Europe

Risks and Challenges

Edited by Thorsten Beck

With contributions from:

Viral Acharya, Joshua Aizenman, Franklin Allen, Thorsten Beck, Erik Berglöf, Claudia Buch, Elena Carletti, Ralph de Haas, Luis Garicano, Andrew Gimber, Charles Goodhart, Vasso Ioannidou, Daniel Gros, Dirk Schoenmaker, Geoffrey Underhill, Wolf Wagner, Benjamin Weigert, Frank Westermann, Charles Wyplosz and Jeromin Zettelmeyer.

CE PR

Centre for Economic Policy Research (CEPR)

The Centre for Economic Policy Research is a network of over 800 Research Fellows and Affiliates, based primarily in European Universities. The Centre coordinates the research activities of its Fellows and Affiliates and communicates the results to the public and private sectors. CEPR is an entrepreneur, developing research initiatives with the producers, consumers and sponsors of research. Established in 1983, CEPR is a European economics research organization with uniquely wide-ranging scope and activities.

The Centre is pluralist and non-partisan, bringing economic research to bear on the analysis of medium- and long-run policy questions. CEPR research may include views on policy, but the Executive Committee of the Centre does not give prior review to its publications, and the Centre takes no institutional policy positions. The opinions expressed in this report are those of the authors and not those of the Centre for Economic Policy Research.

CEPR is a registered charity (No. 287287) and a company limited by guarantee and registered in England (No. 1727026).

Contents

Foreword

Banking regulation and supervision have been key issues of concern and consideration in trying to find appropriate solutions to the problems currently facing the Eurozone, to the extent that the link between sovereign debt and banking risk in Europe was recently described by the European Council as a "vicious cycle" that must be broken. In trying to deal with the challenge of unsustainable cross-border private debt in Europe, the European Commission has recently proposed to establish a more unified banking supervision mechanism in the form of a banking union, which will fall under the auspices of the European Central Bank. However, the road to banking union is beset with many obstacles, not least political intransigence.

This Vox book brings together the views of leading European and US economists on some of those obstacles and offers valuable insights, recommendations and some proposed solutions for the way forward. In his introductory chapter, Thorsten Beck summarises some of the key messages that emerge from the book, such as the importance of recognising that there can be no piecemeal approach to banking union, in that centralising supervision alone at the supra-national level, while leaving bank resolution and recapitalisation at the national level could have an adverse effect. Second, that a banking union should be part of a larger reform package that addresses sovereign fragility and the dangerous entanglement of bank and sovereigns. Another important recommendation of the book is to address the potential conflict between immediate crisis resolution whilst at the same time ensuring that the appropriate structures are in place to enable the many long-term institutional reforms that are now so clearly needed.

During the four years that have elapsed since the collapse of Lehman Brothers in 2008 – an event which heralded the most serious global financial crisis since the 1930s – CEPR's policy portal Vox (www.voxeu.org), under the editorial guidance of Richard Baldwin, has produced 16 books on crisis-related issues written by world-leading economists and specialists. The books have been designed to shed light on the problems related to the crisis and to provide expert advice and guidance for policy makers on potential solutions.

The books are produced rapidly and are timed to catch the wave as the issue under discussion reaches a high point of debate amongst world leaders and decision-makers. The topic of this book is no exception to that pattern in that, on Thursday 18 October 2012, the European Council, involving heads of state or government of the EU Member States and the President of the European Commission, will meet to discuss "progress made on the proposal on a single European banking supervision mechanism and, where necessary, set further orientations. It will also look at the wider issues of banking union and its components". (*http://register.consilium.europa.eu/pdf/en/12/st13/st13386.en12. pdf*)

We are grateful to Thorsten Beck for his enthusiasm and energy in organising and coordinating the inputs to this book; we are also grateful to the authors of the papers for their rapid responses to the invitation to contribute. As ever, we also gratefully acknowledge the contribution of the CEPR Publications Team – Anil Shamdasani and Charlie Anderson – who produced the book with characteristic speed and professionalism.

A solution must be found, and quickly, for Europe's failing banks. As was noted in the last Vox book on *The Future of Banking*, the banking crisis also has potentially massive global implications, in that, if European banks fail then there will be serious problems for Asian and US lenders too. The IMF has recently stated that a banking union in Europe is 'indispensable and must include the critical elements of "a pan-European deposit guarantee scheme, and a pan-European resolution mechanism with common backstops". There are of course many obstacles and challenges, as this book clearly illustrates, but there at least seems to be agreement on the basic concept and necessity of a banking union in Europe.

It is our sincere hope that this book will help to take some of the devil out of the detail and provide policy makers with the insights and perspectives that will enable the rapid but measured process of reforms that must now be implemented in Europe's banking sector.

Viv Davies

Chief Operating Officer, CEPR

15 October 2012

Banking union for Europe – risks and challenges

Thorsten Beck
Tilburg University and CEPR

The Eurozone crisis has gone through its fair share of buzzwords – 'fiscal compact', 'growth compact', 'Big Bazooka', etc. The latest kid on the block is the *banking union*. While discussed by economists since even before the 2007 crisis, it has moved up to the top of the Eurozone agenda. But what kind of banking union? For whom? Financed how? And managed by whom? This new Vox eBook comprises 15 papers on this topic, by leading economists from both sides of the Atlantic.

The authors do not necessarily agree on every single issue and point to several tradeoffs. However, there are several consistent messages coming out of this book:

- No piecemeal approach. Centralising supervision alone at the supranational level, while leaving bank resolution and recapitalisation at the national level, is not only unhelpful but might make things worse!

- A banking union is part of a larger reform package that has to address sovereign fragility and the entanglement of banks with sovereigns.

- Immediate crisis resolution versus long-term reforms. There is an urgent need to address banking and sovereign fragility to resolve the Eurozone crisis. Transitional solutions that deal with legacy problems, both at the bank as at the sovereign level, are urgently needed and can buy sufficient time to implement the many long-term institutional reforms that cannot be introduced immediately.

Addressing the current crisis

The push for a banking union stems from the realisation that the financial safety net for the Eurozone is incomplete. While the original Eurozone structure did not foresee it, the ECB is effectively the lender of last resort, but – as argued by **Charles Wyplosz** – is ill equipped to act as such. First, it has limited information about banks and no authority to intervene. Second, national authorities with the responsibility to intervene, restructure, and recapitalise banks procrastinate as long as possible, putting additional pressure on the ECB to intervene, but only when it is too late. The Spanish case is very illustrative in this context, as discussed by **Luis Garicano**. In order to fully discharge its duties as lender of last resort, the ECB would therefore need not only supervisory but also resolution authority for all Eurozone banks.

Slowly, slowly – I am in a hurry!

Claudia Buch and Benjamin Weigert argue that a banking union should be part of a long-run institutional framework but that the transition is blocked by legacy problems. Therefore, there should be no hasty move toward a banking union, but rather intermediate solutions. Any direct recapitalisation of banks by EFSF and ESM should still turn into liabilities for national governments to match financial and operational responsibility for resolving banks. At the same time, and based on a recent proposal by the German Council of Economic Experts, Buch and Weigert advocate the establishment of a European Redemption Pact that includes joint and several liability for countries' sovereign debt above the threshold of 60%, while also introducing a tightened fiscal compact and a sovereign insolvency regime. This reflects a common theme throughout several of the contributions: banking and sovereign distress have to be tackled at the same time, as they are interlinked in a vicious cycle. This can also help get the ECB out of the fiscal policy realm.

Several authors point out that one should distinguish between solutions to the current crisis and institutional solutions to make the euro a long-term sustainable currency union by constructing a banking union. Using a Eurozone-wide deposit insurance and supervision mechanism to solve legacy problems is like introducing insurance after the insurance case has occurred and also overshadows important changes in the European architecture with distributional conflicts related to crisis resolution. **Thorsten Beck** therefore suggests establishing a crisis resolution mechanism (European Resolution Authority), using the EFSF and ESM as backstop funding sources, while at the same time establishing the necessary structures for a banking union.

The disentangling of banks and sovereign is not limited to the resolution of the current crisis. **Viral Acharya** makes clear that "a fuller solution to the problem of entanglement of sovereign and banking sectors requires not just a banking union in Europe but direct addressing of the sovereign excess in the borrowing markets". This requires adjustments in capital charges for sovereign bonds, and government bonds eligible for liquidity holdings must be in the highest quality bucket and possibly diversified across sovereigns. A point also made by **Wolf Wagner** who calls for diversified sovereign bond holdings of banks or, alternatively, the introduction of synthetic Eurobonds, which are claims on portfolios of Eurozone sovereign bonds. Alternatively, the ECB would have to apply haircuts in taking sovereign debt as collateral in line with the sovereign's credit risk.

Addressing imbalances within the Eurozone

A properly working banking union can also help address the macroeconomic imbalances within the Eurozone. **Daniel Gros** starts from the observation that the desire to protect the home turf in northern Europe has bottled up large amounts of savings there, thus contributing to the severity of the Eurozone crisis. Providing the ECB with supervisory authority could have an important macroeconomic impact because the ECB would not penalise cross-border lending in the way national supervisors do today. Such a move would thus allow the Single European Market in Banking to function again, including intra-bank capital markets, i.e. flows between parent bank and subsidiaries, a critical condition not only to making the credit channel of monetary policy work again, but also restarting growth especially in peripheral countries, and thus dampening the multiplier effect of fiscal policy.

The current debate on banking union can also be directly linked to the recent debate on TARGET2 imbalances, as argued by **Frank Westermann**. The large imbalances in the Eurozone payment system reflect not necessarily deposit flight, but the financing of weak banks in peripheral countries by national central banks, refinanced in turn through the TARGET2 system. This propping up of weak banks by accepting non-marketable securities without the relevant haircuts illustrates again the delay in properly addressing bank and sovereign fragility in peripheral countries, and also shows the urgency to do so. A Eurozone-wide deposit insurance will therefore not be able to stop these imbalances by itself, but has to be accompanied by tackling the bank fragility directly as well as other structural problems in peripheral countries.

Banking union for whom?

One critical question is whether the banking union should be 'just' for the Eurozone or for the whole EU. **Thorsten Beck** argues that the need for a banking union is stronger within a currency union, as it is here where the close link between monetary and financial stability plays out strongest and where the link between government and banking fragility is exacerbated as national governments lack policy tools that countries with an independent monetary policy have available. **Jeromin Zettelmeyer, Erik Berglöf and Ralph de Haas**, on the other hand, argue that non-Eurozone countries should be allowed to opt into the banking union but, if they do so, must be given a say in the governance and access to euro liquidity through swap lines with the ECB. Apart from full membership, intermediate options could be considered which would extend some but not all benefits and obligations of membership to all financially integrated European countries – including countries outside the EU.

While initial proposals posited a banking union only for large, cross-border banks, several authors stress the need to include all banks, including smaller ones. As the example of Spain shows, it may be "the small institutions ... [that] play the role of the canary in the mine in anticipating the systemic problems" (**Luis Garicano**). And if the ECB is to fulfill its role of lender of last resort to all banks, it also needs the authority to supervise and resolve all banks (**Charles Wyplosz**).

The institutional details

Should the responsibilities for running the banking union be concentrated in the ECB? Before deciding to do so, better consult the experiences with central banks managing possible conflicts of interest, argues **Vasso Ioannidou.** There are clear arguments to separate bank resolution and deposit insurance in an institution outside the ECB, to avoid conflicts between monetary and micro-stability goals and introduce an additional monitoring instance (**Dirk Schoenmaker**). One argument for a supranational supervisor is to reduce political capture of regulators that could be observed across Europe over the past years and became obvious during the current crisis. This lesson can also be learnt from Spain, as Luis Garicano points out: "the supervisor must be able and willing to stand up to politicians". In addition, there is a supervisory tendency to be too lenient towards national champions, while bailing them out is too costly, explains **Charles Goodhart. Franklin Allen, Elena Carletti, and Andrew Gimber** argue, however, that the ECB might not necessarily be a tougher supervisor than national authorities. It might actually be more lenient, as it is concerned about contagion across the Eurozone and because it has more resources available. Tying its hands by rules might therefore be necessary.

Several authors, including **Dirk Schoenmaker**, criticise the sequential introduction of supervision and bank resolution, which might lead to less, rather than more, stability, as conflicts between the ECB and the national resolution authorities are bound to arise. Schoenmaker argues for the joint establishment of a strong European supervisor (the

ECB) and a credible European Deposit Insurance and Resolution Authority (EDIRA). Similarly, **Charles Wyplosz** argues that "a partial banking union is no better than no banking union at all, and possibly worse." Without resolution powers, it will find itself forced to inject more and more liquidity and keep the zombies alive. But what about taxpayer back-stop funding; how will such losses distributed across the Eurozone countries? Establishing *ex-ante* rules for burden sharing across countries that 'share' a failing cross-border bank is critical, as pointed out by **Charles Goodhart**.

The crisis has not only exposed political capture of supervisors, but also the risk of supervisory inertia due to career concerns or a 'not-on-my-watch' attitude, a syndrome present certainly not only in Spain, but also in other countries in the Eurozone and beyond. For every failed Spanish *caja*, there is a failed German *Landesbank*. Expanding the supervisory toolbox is not sufficient, supervisory incentives have to be addressed as well, a lesson that goes well beyond our continent!

While a banking union can solve many problems, it might create new sources of systemic risk, argues **Wolf Wagner.** By combining resources, banking fragility in one country can actually more easily drag down the other countries. He therefore argues for a two-tier approach with both national and European insurance in place. The national insurance system will be the first line of defence against domestic crises, while the European fund would serve as backstop funder. A second challenge lies in the harmonisation of supervision and regulation that is likely to come about with a banking union. If all institutions are subject to the same supervisory and regulatory environment, they will tend to undertake similar activities and react in similar ways – also known as herding, which enhances the risk of joint failures.

Looking west across the Atlantic

This time is not different! Studying history can be insightful, for economists as for policymakers. Accordingly, several observers have looked for comparisons in economic history for clues on how to solve the Eurozone crisis. **Joshua Aizenman** argues that the US history suggests large gains from buffering currency unions with a union-wide deposit insurance, and partial debt mutualisation. It is important to note, however, that it took the US a long time to get to where it is now, quite some institutional experimentation and several national banking crises. And as currently discussed in Europe, the US had to address both banking fragility and state overindebtedness. Fiscal union and banking union go hand in hand.

It's the politics, stupid!

In addition to a banking, sovereign, macroeconomic and currency crisis, the Eurozone faces a governance crisis. Diverse interests have hampered an efficient and prompt resolution of the crisis. And as financial support for several peripheral Eurozone countries has involved political conflicts both between and within Eurozone countries, so the discussion on the banking union has an important political economy aspect, **Geoffrey Underhill** points out. More importantly, there is an increasing lack of political legitimacy and sustainability of the Eurozone and for the move towards closer fiscal and banking integration. "Citizens in both creditor and debtor countries increasingly perceive rightly or wrongly that the common currency and perhaps European integration *tout court* have intensified economic risks". A banking union can therefore only succeed with the necessary electoral support to not get further caught in a legitimacy vortex.

This political economy analysis of the Eurozone is consistent with what several authors refer to as the Eurozone's tragedy of the commons problem. It is in the interest of every member government with fragile banks to "share the burden" with the other members, be it through the ECB's liquidity support or the TARGET2 system. Rather than coming up with crisis resolution on the political level, the ECB and the Eurosystem are being used to apply short-term palliatives that deepen distributional problems and make the crisis resolution ultimately more difficult. And at the same time, national supervisory authorities restrict the single banking market further and further, acting out of national interests but ultimately undermining the currency union.

Conclusions

The Eurozone crisis is as much a banking as it is a sovereign debt crisis. Foremost, however, it is a crisis of governance structures and political constraints. The crisis has been exacerbated by half-baked approaches and unsustainable policies. Political inaction has put greater responsibility and stress on the ECB, expanding its realm far beyond monetary stability and its democratically assigned responsibilities, and forcing it to go for second- or third-best solutions. If the Eurozone countries are not to be caught in the downward spiral of a failed currency union, it is time to act now. We economists have certainly made our contribution, showing different alternative paths and policy options. It is time for Eurozone governments to think outside the box and act.

About the author

Thorsten Beck is Professor of Economics and Chairman of the European Banking CentER at Tilburg University. Before joining Tilburg University in 2008, he worked at the Development Research Group of the World Bank. His research and policy work has focused on international banking and corporate finance and has been published in *Journal of Finance*, *Journal of Financial Economics*, *Journal of Monetary Economcis* and *Journal of Economic Growth*. His operational and policy work has focused on Sub-Saharan Africa and Latin America. He is also Research Fellow at the Centre for Economic Policy Research (CEPR) in London and a Fellow in the Center for Financial Studies in Frankfurt. He studied at Tübingen University, Universidad de Costa Rica, University of Kansas and University of Virginia.

Banking union as a crisis-management tool

Charles Wyplosz
Graduate Institute, Geneva, ICMB and CEPR

Countries have various mechanisms that provide lending when a bank fails. But when bank problems far exceed available resources, central banks must be lenders of last resort, even when their role is clouded to mitigate moral hazard. This column explains the ECB is ill-equipped to act as such a lender; it doesn't have enough control due to coordination problems across countries. The column argues this must change. The ECB must be the lender of last resort and this involves a Eurozone banking union.

There can be no banking system without a lender of last resort. Some countries have various mechanisms that provide lending in first resort when a bank fails. This can be a deposit insurance agency, a rainy day fund fed by bank dues, or an understanding that banks rescue each other when the need arises. But large banks or a collection of small banks typically have balance sheets that far exceed available resources. This is why central banks must be lenders of last resort, even when their role is clouded in constructive ambiguity to mitigate moral hazard.

Bank crises do not just involve lenders in first and last resort. Sizeable sums of money cannot be injected into a black hole. The authorities must have complete and up-to-date knowledge of each bank so that they can detect whether and how much money is needed in the case of failure. Because this is taxpayers' money, the authorities must be able to determine the viability of a failing bank and, if needed, how to proceed to shut it down with minimal impact on depositors and other creditors, including deciding which creditors need protection and which should bear losses alongside shareholders. Because bank crises are often explosive and sometimes threaten to spread throughout the banking and financial sector, the decisions must sometimes be made in a matter of hours. The authorities must always be ready and perfectly informed. This is the role of supervisors and of the resolution authority that may be called upon to restructure or close the banks down.

While the details vary, all developed countries and many emerging market countries have developed such institutions. This is also the case in the Eurozone countries, and this is a major problem. As noted by Begg et al. (1998), with one central bank, Eurozone countries need one regulator, one supervisor, and one resolution authority, not N of them, where N is the number of member countries.

Like many other central banks, the ECB has always insisted that it is not a lender of last resort. The usual reason is that central banks wish to avoid giving commercial banks an implicit bailout insurance that would encourage risky behaviour. It is understood, however, that the central bank would step in if a serious bank crisis were to occur. But this is not the case of the ECB, for two good reasons at least.

First, the ECB has limited real-time knowledge of the situation of banks. Information can be requested but it will filter through national supervision authorities whose first allegiance is to their governments. High potential costs of a bank failure, closeness with banks, and protectionist feelings are likely to limit the free flow of information to the ECB. In addition, the ECB has no authority to close insolvent banks or even to design restructuring plans. Intervening as lender of last resort, the ECB would provide money without any control.

Second, lending in last resort can be costly; the ECB could suffer losses. In one country, whether the losses occur at the central bank or at the treasury makes little difference since the taxpayers are always the residual burden bearers. Within the Eurozone, ECB losses are borne by taxpayers from all member countries. The European Treaty stipulates that the ECB would intervene on behalf of the authorities of the failing bank, who would be responsible for any losses. The arrangement can work in the case of one bank with no cross-border activities. However, cross-border activities – encouraged to promote a single financial market – would open up litigations. In addition, the relevant government may be unable to live up to its legal obligation if it is already under pressure because of its own indebtedness.

The result is particularly disturbing, with many features of a Nash outcome remindful of the tragedy of the commons. It is in the interest of every member government with fragile banks to 'share the burden' with the other members. Given the size of the amounts potentially involved, national authorities have a strong interest to deny that any national bank is in difficulty for as long as possible, until the costs are so large that a central bank intervention becomes necessary. After the rescue, the authorities have a further interest in protecting its bank from being broken down as part of a resolution whose costs, if any, could be shared. Knowing this, the ECB has every reason to seek to avoid getting involved. Yet, when the costs exceed resources available to governments, the ECB cannot stand aside as a national banking system unravels, with a high probability of contagion to other countries.

This is why, in spite of the constructive ambiguity that some want to retain, the ECB must be recognised as the lender of last resort to Eurozone banks. At the very least, it must be accepted that there may exist crisis situations when the ECB will have to intervene, and consequences ought to be drawn. These consequences are that the Eurozone needs a single regulator, a single supervisor, a single resolution authority and, most likely, a common deposit insurance mechanism. This is what defines a banking union.

A banking union is politically difficult to fathom. It involves a transfer of competence from national to Eurozone authorities. It entails apparent income redistribution among countries. It requires the setting up of new institutions. Its need is only apparent at crisis time, even though its existence is bound to change incentives of both banks and governments. The consequences of these changing incentives are unpalatable to banks in quiet times inasmuch as they result in less risk-taking and less profits.

The clash between the required coherence of what has to be done and the predictable political opposition is particularly worrisome. At the current stage of the crisis, most Eurozone banks are not seen as close to failing. The Irish and Spanish wake-up calls have brought home the need for a banking union of some sort, but the threat of a systemic banking crisis remains remote. It matters little that good policymaking requires planning for the worst, resistance is bound to be strong as long as most countries feel safe. The risk is to adopt some but not all the measures that are part of the definition of a banking union.

Indeed, the proposal that the European Commission has put forth in early September 2012 only includes regulation and supervision. Resolution and a deposit insurance mechanism are postponed. Even worse, a number of governments want to strictly limit the number of banks that would fall under the European supervisor's authority and to delay the project. The very same reasons and actors that blocked any discussion of these issues at the time when the Maastricht Treaty was under negotiation are back in action.

It is essential to understand that a partial banking union is no better than no banking union at all, and possibly worse. Imagine that we only have a single regulator and that the common supervisor only looks at large banks. Imagine that a series of governments, small and large, restructure their public debts, an occurrence that many regard as unavoidable. Because banks typically hold large amounts of national bonds, a public-debt restructuring is likely to cause deep losses in small and large banks. The 2007-8 scenario has amply shown how mutual suspicion promptly steps in and brings the interbank market to a halt. The ECB must then provide liquidity to individual banks, small and large. In addition, some banks may fail, bringing along others. The ECB is facing its role as lending in last resort. If it only supervises large banks, it cannot provide liquidity and, if need be, emergency assistance to the smaller banks. Financially hard-pressed governments will need to provide resources that they do not possess and cannot even borrow. Healthier governments may start down the road followed by Ireland and Spain and find themselves losing market access as well. Large banks too will be engulfed. With no resolution authority, the ECB will not feel able to inject amounts that could reach several trillions of euros. Apocalypse now.

This is a scenario, of course. It is not just plausible, it is reasonably probable.

References

Begg, D, P de Grauwe, F Giavazzi, H Uhlig and C Wyplosz (1998), 'The ECB: Safe at Any Speed?', *Monitoring the European Central Bank* 1, CEPR.

About the author

Charles Wyplosz is Professor of International Economics at the Graduate Institute, Geneva, where he is Director of the International Centre for Money and Banking Studies. Previously, he has served as Associate Dean for Research and Development at INSEAD and Director of the PhD program in Economics at the Ecole des Hautes Etudes en Science Sociales in Paris. He is a CEPR Research Fellow and has served as Director of the International Macroeconomics Programme at CEPR.

Legacy problems in transition to a banking union

Claudia M Buch and Benjamin Weigert

Tübingen University, IAW and German Council of Economic Experts; German Council of Economic Experts

As a banking union within the Eurozone seems ever more likely, this column looks at banking union as a way of responding to the crisis, but also as a way of preventing the next one.

1.   Background

At their June 2012 summit, the heads of state of the Eurozone have decided upon policy measures that aim at breaking the "vicious circle between banks and sovereigns". Most importantly, the summit declaration envisages the establishment of a single supervisory mechanism involving the ECB. Given that the supervisory mechanism has been established, the ESM shall be allowed to recapitalise banks directly. Establishment of a single supervisory mechanism would be an important step towards a banking union consisting of pan-European supervision, restructuring and resolution, and deposit insurance. Hence, a banking union is a long-term project which is part of a new institutional structure for Europe.

Such a new long-run institutional framework should rest on three pillars (GCEF 2010, 2011): A substantially enhanced Stability and Growth Pact including strict fiscal rules and an insolvency regime for sovereigns, a unified pan-European financial regulation and supervision with a wide range of effective instruments and, finally, a European Crisis Mechanism which is directly linked to the insolvency regime for sovereigns.

Just as many other elements of this new institutional structure, steps towards a banking union are blocked by legacy problems. As a result of an overexpansion of private and public sector debt in the run-up to the crisis, the Eurozone faces three severe and closely interrelated crises: a sovereign debt crisis, a banking crisis, and a macroeconomic crisis. These crises are mutually reinforcing, thus culminating in a crisis of confidence.

Legacy problems obstruct the transition to a new long-run institutional structure in many ways. For example, enforcing the Fiscal Compact would require significant improvements in fiscal indicators in some countries. In addition, as long as banks carry non-performing assets on their balance sheets and as long as losses on these assets have not fully been acknowledged, introducing pan-European deposit insurance would amount to the introduction of an insurance system after the insured event has already happened. This would entail severe moral hazard problems. Hence, a consistent and credible framework for bank resolution and restructuring must be a core element of a banking union. Yet, progress towards financial sector reform to date has been slow, and key elements of the reform package are unlikely to be introduced in the near future. In this sense, 'legacy' problems not only refer to debt overhang but also to delayed financial sector reforms.

The German Council of Economic Experts (2011, 2012), has recently outlined steps towards dealing with legacy problems in the banking system and with excess debt burdens of the public sector. In the following, we summarise the main conclusions. For a full version see GCEE (2012).

2.   Dealing with distressed banks

Many banks in the crisis countries are in distress and carry a high share of non-performing assets on their balance sheets. The resulting banking sector distress can have severe negative implications for the real sector and for financial stability. Banks carrying non-performing assets on their balance sheets have incentives to gamble for resurrection, which can prevent an efficient reallocation of assets from shrinking to growing sectors of the economy. Japan's experience in the 1990s and 2000s constitutes a prime example of the wrong incentives that delayed recapitalisation and restructuring of banks can have for the real economy (Caballero et al. 2008).

These developments do not only affect individual countries. Due to foreign trade and financial linkages, banking distress can have negative spillover effects for the entire Eurozone. Low confidence in banks in the distressed countries has caused private capital inflows to dry up or even to reverse. Many banks in these countries are no longer able to refinance themselves through the private capital market and are strongly reliant on financing through the ECB. The ECB has lowered standards for central bank-eligible collateral and has provided liquidity assistance. All this is reflected in a sharp rise in TARGET2 balances within the Eurosystem. All EMU member states are liable for the risks that are shifted onto the central bank's balance sheet.

In short, the European banking and financial sector is in an acute crisis that calls for swift action by policymakers. At the same time, delayed financial sector reforms are hampering crisis management. Essentially, the statement of the June 2012 summit rightly focuses on the links between banks and sovereigns. What will be decisive are the concrete measures to be taken and the speed with which the necessary reforms are implemented.

2.1. Acute crisis management

Currently, banking sector problems are most pressing in Spain. Spain has already applied for funding to recapitalise its banks from the EFSF, and it has signed a corresponding Memorandum of Understanding. A solution to problems in the Spanish banking sector cannot wait until a fully-fledged long-term regulatory framework for the European banking system has been established. At the same time, clear conditions under which funds for bank recapitalisation in Spain will be used need to be specified. Experience with banking sector restructuring in the past can provide useful guidance how to proceed – and which mistakes to avoid. Generally, recapitalisation of banks through public funds should not lead to government ownership of banks in the long term. On the contrary, recapitalisation through the government should enable the banks to regain health as quickly as possible, to reduce costs for taxpayers and to restore a functioning banking system by re-privatising the banks.

To achieve these goals, recapitalisation and restructuring must follow clear criteria. First, on the basis of a thorough audit of banks' balance sheets with the assistance of outside experts, banks' capital requirements must be defined. Second, only if these capital requirements cannot be covered from private or from national sources could EFSF or ESM loans be granted to the government. The government should be liable for funds used for bank recapitalisation. Clear conditionality needs to be imposed. Third, the government should provide additional equity capital, and it should assume the associated control functions. The goal must be to restructure banks in such a way that they have sustainable business models in the future. It will be necessary to closely involve European institutions and specifically the European competition authorities in the process.

Should it be necessary to resort to the EFSF or the ESM to recapitalise banks, the government should be liable for these funds. The conditions stipulated in the June 2012 statement by the EMU heads of state and government allow for direct recapitalisation to banks *only* if a European supervisory mechanism has been established. In the meantime, the EU Commission has outlined the concept of such a Single Supervisory Mechanism. The timeline foresees a sequence, starting with supervision of banks applying for funding from the EFSF/ESM by the ECB in January 2013. Given the scope and scale of the required regulatory changes, this time line seems overly ambitious. Hence, the conditions for funding to be granted directly to the banks without the government assuming liability will not be met in the foreseeable future. Moreover, supervision at the European level does not in itself suffice. Instead, powers of restructuring and resolution must be transferred to a European-level body as well.

2.2.   Make up for lost time

In the longer term, an effective supervisor at the European level should ensure that the probability and the scale of crises decline. Higher bank capital will play a key role in this context because this will enhance the banks' ability to bear risk. Parallel to this, effective mechanisms for restructuring and winding up banks need to be established. The implementation of common supervisory and resolution mechanisms should be a precondition for using common financial resources to restructure banks.

In the past four years since the outbreak of the financial crisis, key financial market reforms have been discussed in Europe. However, only a few have been initiated. Coherent implementation is still missing. At present, finding a comprehensive solution to the European debt crisis is complicated by the absence of an effective and European-wide procedure for restructuring and winding up banks. This affects, in particular, large and systemically important credit institutions with significant cross-border activities. Priority should therefore be given to reforms in these areas.

2.3.   No hasty moves towards a banking union

Establishing a banking union will take a considerable amount of time. Key issues to be clarified include the questions of how to involve the central bank into the supervisory process while clearly separating monetary policy functions, how to define the exact tasks of the European and the national banking supervisors, how to introduce uniform processes for winding up and restructuring banks, and not least how to solve the attendant financing questions. A long-term system in which liability and control are closely linked requires not least that national sovereignty is partly given up. This will invariably take some time. It is therefore all the more important that progress is made now on introducing the regulatory changes required.

3.   Dealing with distressed sovereigns

Legacy problems do not only affect the banking system. Recurring instabilities on markets for government debt also show the need to deal with distressed sovereigns. The Fiscal Compact, which has been agreed upon by 25 EU member countries in February 2012, is the right and necessary step towards fiscal consolidation and debt reduction. It is, therefore, an indispensable element of the long-term stability framework in the Eurozone. But to make the Fiscal Compact a credible framework in the short and medium run, countries need both strong economic growth and sustainable levels of interest rates. Yet risk premia even on long-term Italian and Spanish government bonds have risen considerably compared with German bonds. Hence, contagion has spread to countries that were previously regarded by financial markets as fiscally solid and undoubtedly solvent. Because (short-term) interest rates can be influenced by the ECB, the ECB is under immense pressure to support fiscal policy of indebted countries, which is in conflict with its mandate of delivering price stability to the Eurozone.

3.1.   ECB trapped in the fiscal realm

Unconventional monetary policy measures taken by the ECB have helped to stabilise the situation. The ECB has provided banks in the Eurozone with extensive liquidity for the next three years at very favourable conditions, it has expanded its collateral framework of eligible assets for refinancing operations, and it has recently introduced the Outright Monetary Transaction program with conditionality attached to an EFSF/ESM program. While these measures aim at breaking the link between banks and sovereigns, transactions in secondary sovereign bond markets are dangerously close to the monetisation of sovereign debt. Stabilisation thus comes at a very high price. The politically well-established division between fiscal policy and monetary policy has been successively blurred. Phasing out unconventional measures in the near future will be very difficult. If changing market sentiments or inactivity of European fiscal authorities will lead to a renewed intensification of the crisis, there will be immense pressure on the ECB to step in once more. Hence, the key issue is to find a fiscal solution to a stabilisation of sovereign bond markets.

3.2. The European Redemption Pact proposal

With the introduction of the EFSF and the ESM, fiscal policymakers have implemented a firewall. However, in the current crisis, the shortcoming of the ESM is that it acts *ex post*, that it cannot and should not be used as a preventive measure, and that it is not designed to deal with fiscal legacy problems (Buch 2012). The Fiscal Compact that addresses fiscal consolidation and debt reduction lacks credibility because, in the current economic environment, the consolidation path is highly unrealistic for many countries. Therefore, in November 2011, the German Council of Economic Experts proposed the European Redemption Pact (ERP) as a crisis resolution mechanism that provides a viable bridge to the long-term stability framework (GCEE 2011; Doluca et al. 2012).

The ERP consists of three contiguous elements: a tightened Fiscal Compact together with its prescribed fiscal consolidation paths, a European Redemption Fund (ERF) for sovereign debt in excess of 60% of GDP providing limited and temporary joint and several liability, and a sovereign insolvency regime which becomes effective after all excessive debt has been redeemed. The main objective of the proposal is to restore national responsibility for fiscal policy in line with the revised and tightened SGP and the no-bail-out clause of the Lisbon treaty.

Strict safeguards against moral hazard are the backbone of the ERP. As a prerequisite for joining the ERP, countries need to ratify the Fiscal Compact and to introduce national debt brakes. Compliance with national debt brakes should be monitored by an independent European body that would also impose penalty payments to the ERF in case of any violations. Participation is restricted to countries that are not already on under an adjustment program of the EFSF/ESM (i.e., Greece, Portugal, Ireland, and Cyprus would not participate). These countries are allowed to outsource that part of their sovereign debt to the ERF that exceeds, at a pre-specified date, the threshold of 60% debt-to-GDP ratio being set out in line with the Maastricht Treaty. The outsourcing of sovereign debt to the ERF is stretched over a multi-year time horizon until the predefined volume of debt is reached (roll-in phase) (Figure 1). During this period, the ERF will buy a country's long-term bonds (with maturity over two years) on the primary market while any short term debt is still issued on the financial market.

The ERF interest rates for any debt transferred are expected to be significantly lower than what markets currently demand from countries like Italy or Spain. In return, participating countries would enter into payment obligations towards the ERF that are calculated such that each country would repay its transferred debt within 25 years. After this period, the ERF would dissolve itself. All participating countries are jointly and severally liable for any debt transferred to the ERF. Therefore, the ERP has a lot of strings attached, and it entails a sanctioning mechanism to ensure a successful transition to sound public finances.

Figure 1 Debts in European Redemption Fund by country (€ billion)

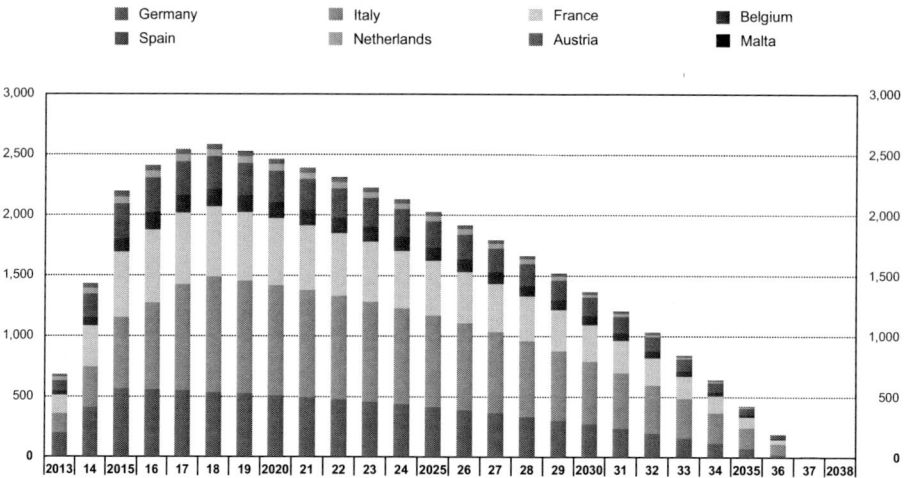

Notes: 1) Own calculations as of June 2012. Assumed starting date of the ERP: 1.1.2013; basic data: European Commission, AMECO database, 26.7.2012.

3.3.   Preventive measures with strict conditionality

Outsourcing of debt is tied to strict conditionality. Countries need to comply with consolidation plans that are agreed upon by participating countries at the time of joining the ERP. In case of non-compliance, various sanctions can be imposed on the country that range from interest rate mark-ups for debt already transferred to the fund to complete suspension of the roll-in phase.

To limit moral hazard and to limit the joint and several liability borne by participating countries, each country has to pledge collateral – currency or gold reserves or covered bonds – totalling 20% of the debt outsourced to the ERF. The collateral would automatically accrue to the fund if a country does not meet its payment obligations. Additionally, countries have to politically earmark certain (new) taxes that are used to meet the payment obligations.

One of the decisive features of the ERF is that it does not completely substitute the markets' disciplining effects. During the roll-in phase, governments still have to rely on financial markets to refinance their short-term debt. After the roll-in phase, a country has to refinance the remaining debt of up to 60% of GDP and is, therefore, fully exposed to market discipline.

The goal of the ERP is to address the systemic crisis of confidence by a credible political commitment to the Euro. But the ERP is certainly no panacea, and it entails risks. Therefore, the proposal must be assessed against the alternatives. Dealing with legacy problems is, by no means, a trivial task, and it involves decisions with redistributive implications to be taken. Advantages of the ERP are that it makes the true scale of the risks assumed by creditor countries transparent, that any assistance provided is subject to strict conditionality, and that redistributive decisions are democratically legitimated. This is a crucial feature which distinguishes the ERP from de facto debt mutualisation through the ECB. The ERP also restores the separation of monetary and fiscal policy, and it provides breathing space so that country-specific structural problems can be overcome.

References

Buch, C M (2012), 'From the Stability Pact to ESM - What next?', in A. Dombret and O Lucius (eds.) *Stability of the Financial System - Illusion or Feasible Concept?* (forthcoming) and IAW Discussion Papers 85, Institut für Angewandte Wirtschaftsforschung (IAW). Tuebingen.

Caballero, R J T Hoshi und Anil K Kashyap (2008), 'Zombie Lending and Depressed Restructuring in Japan', *American Economic Review* 98(5): 1943–77.

Doluca, H, M Hübner, D Rumpf, and B Weigert (2012), 'The European Redemption Pact: Implementation and macroeconomic effects', *Intereconomics: Review of European Economic Policy*, 230-239, vol. 47(4).

German Council of Economic Experts (GCEF) (2010), Annual Report 2011/2012 'Chances for a stable upturn'. Wiesbaden.

German Council of Economic Experts (GCEF) (2011), Annual Report 2011/2012 "Assume responsibility for Europe", Wiesbaden.

German Council of Economic Experts (GCEF) (2012), Special Report 'After the Euro Area Summit: Time to Implement Long-term Solutions', Wiesbaden.

About the authors

Claudia M Buch joined the University of Tübingen in 2004, where she holds the chair for International Macroeconomics and Finance. On March 1, 2012, she was appointed member of the German Council of Economic Experts. She has been the Scientific Director of the Institute for Applied Economic Research (Tübingen) since January 2005. She is a member of the Scientific Advisory Council to the German Ministry of Economics, of the Advisory Scientific Committee to the European Systemic Risk Board (ESRB), and of the extended board of directors of the German Economic Association. From 1992 to 2003, Claudia Buch was affiliated with the Kiel Institute for World Economics (Germany) where she headed the research area "Financial Markets". She graduated from the University of Bonn, Germany, with a Master of Economics in 1991 and from the University of Wisconsin with a Master of Business Administration in 1989. From the University of Kiel, she received a PhD in Economics in 1996 and a Habilitation (German post-doc degree) in 2002. She has published widely on issues related to international finance and macroeconomics, international financial markets, financial integration, international banking, and foreign direct investment.

Benjamin Weigert studied economics at the Technical University of Dresden with a focus on International Economics, Managerial Economics and Econometrics. He received his diploma degree in 2002. In 2007, he received his PhD from the University of Konstanz in International Economics and completed the doctoral program "Quantitative Economics and Finance". He worked as a research assistant at the Chair of Economic Theory in Konstanz from 2002 until 2004 and at the Chair of International Economics in Giessen from 2004 to 2007. After graduation, he joined Deloitte & Touche and worked in offices in Frankfurt, Duesseldorf and Bratislava until 2009. From July 2009 to July 2011, he worked as an economist at the German Council of Economic Experts. Since August 2011 he is Secretary General of the GCEE. He has published on issues of international trade, foreign direct investment, and labour markets.

Why the rush? Short-term crisis resolution and long-term bank stability

Thorsten Beck
Tilburg University and CEPR

The Eurozone crisis has shown that the traditional approach of EU supervisory cooperation is not enough. This column argues the gaps in cross-border bank regulations have to be addressed on three levels: A short-term crisis resolution mechanism for the Eurozone, a functioning banking union, and stronger cooperation agreements across the EU and beyond. Critically, such reforms have to start from the resolution component.

The recent crisis has exposed a critical gap in financial safety nets across Europe and many other developed countries, i.e. a deficient if not absent bank resolution framework. This gap in the financial safety net has become even more critical in the case of cross-border banks. The crisis has shown that the traditional approach of home-host country supervisory cooperation in the form of Memorandums of Understanding and Colleges of Supervisors falls short in case of bank failures. Memorandums of Understanding are non-binding documents and have turned out to be very patient paper. Colleges of Supervisors make for good coordination in good times, but break down in crises, because the ultimate decision is with the home-country supervisor, especially in the case of branches, and the representative of one major stakeholder – the minister of finance on behalf of taxpayers – is typically not included in these colleges. As any national reform of the financial safety net has to improve the resolution component, any reform of the regulatory framework for cross-border banking should start from the resolution part. Not only is bank failure the moment when cooperation between home and host countries is most important, a properly designed resolution framework can also set important incentives against excessively aggressive risk-taking by *banks ex-ante*. Critically, the bank resolution framework has to contain both feasible options for resolving failing banks as well as sufficient funding for covering possible shortfalls. On the national level, resolution and recovery plans and the creation of possible bank resolution funds are therefore being discussed or even implemented.

A new regulatory framework for cross-border banking

On the cross-border level, this might involve a move from college of supervisors to a college of bank resolution authorities that include all relevant parties of the financial safety net, including ministries of finance. This should also include *ex-ante* burden-sharing agreements. For large systemically important financial institutions, this can also include resolution and recovery plans jointly commissioned and supervised by the relevant home and host country supervisors and resolution authorities. The example of the Nordic-Baltic agreement goes in this direction by including all relevant authorities within a college and outlining a specific burden sharing formula. It is interesting to note that this has been agreed upon in a region with not only high cross-border links in banking, but also a long joint history and culture. Such agreements can go a long way towards reducing incentive problems arising from the mismatch of banks' and regulatory geographic perimeters (Beck et al. 2013), as well as the higher risk of systemic failure since cross-border banking increases the similarities of banks across countries and their interconnectedness (Wagner 2010).

The construction of a joint supranational supervisor is trickier for larger areas. While colleges can be created for individual banks, a supranational supervisor might not be relevant for all banks in her specific perimeter of authority. Also, different legal systems, and political opposition to yielding 'sovereignty' over a sensitive sector, such as banking, might make the establishment of a supranational supervisor difficult if not impossible. This sheds doubt on the feasibility and desirability of an EU wide supranational supervisor, which would be responsible for 27 countries with different legal cultures and regulatory systems, and very different financial systems.

A banking union can strengthen the euro

Compared to the EU at large or the global financial system, the Eurozone faces additional challenges in terms of cross-border banking. The recent crisis has shown the close linkages between monetary and financial stability (Allen et al. 2011). While monetary policy should take into account asset and not only consumer-price inflation, one tool is simply not enough to achieve both goals, especially not in a currency union, where asset price cycles are not completely synchronised across countries. In addition, the close link between governments and banks through government bond holdings by banks, while banks at the same time might have to rely on governments for support in crises, is exacerbated in a currency union, where certain policy tools are no longer available to national policymakers. A third problem is that of regulatory and political capture, where regulators get too close to the regulated entities and/or are influenced by politicians in the regulatory process, be they national or local government authorities (see Garicano in this volume for a discussion in the context of Spain). This is exacerbated by the tragedy of commons, referred to by other contributors to this eBook (Frank Westermann, Charles Wyplosz), whereby national authorities are interested in sharing the burden of bank failure with other members of the currency union.

To address these concerns, there have been increasing calls for a banking union. While initial suggestions were for large cross-border banks to be regulated under separate supranational legislation and a supranational supervisory and resolution authority (e.g. Fonteyne et al. 2010), the more recent proposals have been for all banks within the Eurozone to fall under Eurozone-wide regulation and supervision. This is also in recognition that the interaction between monetary and financial stability goes as much through small banks as through large cross-border banks. Take the example of the Spanish *cajas* who are at the core of the vicious cycle between sovereign and bank fragility in Spain. Similarly, the banks with some of the most toxic exposure to cross-border claims in Germany were *Landesbanken* or smaller specialised lenders (e.g., Hypo Real).

These arguments imply that a banking union that complements the currency union should not only focus on cross-border banks, but on all banks. It does not imply that supervision is centralised in one institution; rather it means that the ultimate responsibility lies at the supranational level – the buck stops at the Eurozone level. The critical issue is that the establishment of a supranational supervisory authority alone will not be sufficient. Rather, and in line with the arguments above, bank resolution, i.e. both the powers and the resources to be able to intervene in failing banks is critical for the success of such a banking union, as also argued by Dirk Schoenmaker and others in this eBook. The exact institutional structure and distribution of responsibilities across different institutions goes beyond the scope of this column, but the critical issue is that powers and resources to intervene failing banks have to go hand-in-hand. Independence of the institution from both political sphere and from the regulated entities is critical.

One additional advantage of a banking union could be that the resolution framework can be constructed on the European level and therefore leaves more resolution options that can involve the private sector. A bank that is too big for the Netherlands to resolve without bailout might well be of a reasonable size for a banking union.

Long-term reforms, short-term needs

While some see banking union as crisis-management tool, to address the current widespread private and public-sector overindebtedness in many peripheral countries, there are several reasons to not use it this way. First, building up the necessary structures for a Eurozone regulatory and bank resolution framework cannot be done overnight, while the crisis needs immediate attention. Second, the current discussion on banking union is overshadowed by distributional discussions, as bank fragility is heavily concentrated in the peripheral countries. This can also be seen as the motivation for the retraction by several northern governments of an agreement achieved in June that the European Stability Mechanism would fund bank resolution and recapitalisation in several peripheral countries, most prominently Spain, directly, to thus break the link between bank and sovereign fragility. Starting a new EU institution with such a large redistributional character at the startup seems unwise both for economic and political reasons.

Constructing a banking union will take a long time; the resolution of the current crisis, on the other hand, has already taken too much time. The US has shown how aggressively addressing bank fragility can turn banks from a source of crisis into a potential source of recovery. Europe, on the other hand, has muddled through, with semi-strong stress tests and much leeway for recapitalisation. National sovereign budget restrictions have further delayed recognition and resolution of bank fragility. Together with Daniel Gros and Dirk Schoenmaker, I have therefore suggested the establishment of a temporary European Resolution Authority, for which the ECB can make staff and offices available (Beck et al. 2012). This Resolution Authority would sort out fragile banks across Europe, both small and large; strongly capitalised banks go ahead; and weak banks are either recapitalised or (partly) liquidated. Where possible banks should be recapitalised through the market; if not feasible, the Resolution Authority recapitalises by taking an equity stake in the bank (by straight equity or hybrid securities). The resolution authority, however, would need a fiscal backstop from the European Stability Mechanism to gain the necessary credibility not only with the banks it is tasked to restructure but also with the markets. This resolution authority would be specifically tasked with addressing the current banking crisis, while at the same time the necessary structures for a supranational bank supervisory and resolution authority would be built up.

Conclusions

I have argued that the topic of banking union contains three very different dimensions. First, there is the immediate need for crisis resolution. Together and interlinked with sovereign fragility, bank fragility is at the centre of the current crisis. Recognising losses and allocating them, while separating bank and sovereign crises is the most immediate task to resolve the crisis. A sound and efficient banking system is an important component of the growth compact European politicians have been discussing. Resolving the banking crisis is therefore critical for the Eurozone. Second, there is the medium-term task to strengthen the currency union with a banking union. Monetary and financial stability are too closely interlinked to leave bank regulation and supervision completely on the national level. Third, there is the need for broader reforms of cross-border regulatory cooperation, which should focus on the resolution component and should imply stronger *ex-ante* commitments for the resolution of large cross-border banks. This agenda goes beyond the Eurozone and even beyond the EU.

References

Allen, F, T Beck, E Carletti, P Lane, D Schoenmaker and W Wagner (2011), *Cross-border Banking in Europe: Implications for Financial Stability and Macroeconomic Policies*, CEPR, London.

Beck, T, D Gros and D Schoenmaker (2012), 'Banking Union instead of Eurobonds-disentangling sovereign and banking crises'. VoxEU. 24 June 2012.

Beck, T, R Todorov and W Wagner (2013), 'Supervising Cross-Border Banks: Theory, Evidence and Policy,' *Economic Policy*, forthcoming.

Fonteyne, W, W Bossu, L Cortavarria-Checkley, A Giustiniani, A Gullo, D Hardy and S Kerr (2010), 'Crisis Management and Resolution for a European Banking System', IMF Working Paper 10/70.

Wagner, W (2010), 'Diversification at Financial Institutions and Systemic Crises', *Journal of Financial Intermediation* 19, 272-86.

About the author

Thorsten Beck is Professor of Economics and Chairman of the European Banking CentER at Tilburg University. Before joining Tilburg University in 2008, he worked at the Development Research Group of the World Bank. His research and policy work has focused on international banking and corporate finance and has been published in *Journal of Finance*, *Journal of Financial Economics*, *Journal of Monetary Economcis* and *Journal of Economic Growth*. His operational and policy work has focused on Sub-Saharan Africa and Latin America. He is also Research Fellow in the Centre for Economic Policy Research (CEPR) in London and a Fellow in the Center for Financial Studies in Frankfurt. He studied at Tübingen University, Universidad de Costa Rica, University of Kansas and University of Virginia.

Banking union in Europe and other reforms

Viral V Acharya
NYU Stern School of Business and CEPR

With most of the debate around banking union in the Eurozone focusing primarily on the financial institutions it will regulate, this column argues that the issue of sovereign debt of the members of the Eurozone needs also to be taken into account.

Many observers have rightly noted that problems in the banking system have been at the core of the ongoing European crisis. In response, policymakers in Europe have proposed a banking union. In particular, the European Commission has proposed that the *European Central Bank* have broad authority over all banks within the supervisory mechanism (Veron 2012). While other articles in this eBook book will focus on additional aspects of banking union that are critical to its success (such as adequate and centralised resolution authority for unwinding of banks), I want to highlight in this note the importance of dealing with sovereign debts of member countries in the Eurozone.

The European banking system is heavily entangled with the debt of its member countries, and the bank exposure to troubled countries (Greece, Italy, Portugal, Spain and Ireland) has led to a loss of confidence in the banking system. Such entanglement, on the one hand, creates credibility for banks and other creditors of sovereigns that other countries and the IMF may come readily to the rescue in case of increase in sovereign credit risk. On the other hand, if sovereign credit risk increases to a point whereby political will elsewhere to support the sovereign becomes doubtful, it leads to severe downward revision concerning the health of the banking system. *Ex ante*, the banking system may be prepared to take this downside risk, especially if it is highly undercapitalised to start with (so that exposure to troubled sovereigns becomes an attractive version of a 'carry trade'), or if domestic banks wish to ensure their failure is in a systemic state (downside risk for the entire economy) rather than an idiosyncratic one.[1]

While a banking union and credible resolution authority would mitigate one side of this problem – that undercapitalised banks engage in seeking sovereign credit risk – if sovereigns are keen to borrow more, e.g., to continue with fiscal excesses or covering-up of underlying lack of productivity in the private sector with an expansion of the government balance sheet, then the entanglement may readily arise again in future. Sovereigns could resist revisiting the zero risk-weights for their debt in bank capital requirements, making it attractive for banks to hold their debt as a way of enhancing levered equity return. Liquidity requirements which are aimed as a prudential tool for banking stability may, somewhat perversely, become an easy mechanism for channeling deposits to fund government deficits. The pressure on central banks to lend reserves against all sovereign debt as collateral can attach liquidity properties to sovereign debt that make its yield low even for sovereigns on path of unsustainable deficits.

Hence a fuller solution to the problem of entanglement of sovereign and banking sectors requires not just a banking union in Europe but direct addressing of the sovereign excess in the borrowing markets. Some reforms that may help facilitate this are straightforward and should be brought to the table in policy discussions of the European Commission, the ECB, the European Banking Authority, and other relevant bodies:

1. Sovereign debt risk weights should be adequately sensitive to the risk of the under-
    lying sovereign, and not be allowed to 'race to the bottom' due to lack of participa-
    tion of some countries in such a revision. Some sanctions in the form of restricted
    single-market access for banks of sovereigns that do not participate in a revised
    sovereign risk-weight scheme may be necessary.

---

1   For the role of entanglement of sovereign debt with banks as a commitment device for the sovereign to repay non-bank creditors, see Acharya and Rajan 2011. For empirical evidence consistent with bank exposures in the Eurozone to GIPSIs being a form of "carry trade", see Acharya and Steffen 2012. And, for theoretical and empirical discussion of the two-way feedback between banking sector and sovereign credit risks, see Acharya et al 2011.

2. Liquidity requirements in bank regulation should similarly not treat all sovereign debt holdings as identical regardless of the sovereign's credit risk. The eligible liquidity holdings must be in the highest quality bucket and possibly diversified across sovereigns whose debt qualifies for this bucket.

3. The ECB should make the haircuts in taking sovereign debt as collateral in line with the sovereign's credit risk, and in fact, require minimum solvency criteria for sovereigns for their debt to qualify as eligible collateral. To the extent that such haircuts are likely to come under duress in a crisis situation, a rule-based approach with discretion primarily to revise downward the eligibility of risky sovereign debt may be needed.

All of the approaches above suffer from the problem that sovereign credit risk may alter swiftly as it did in 2008-09 due to revelation of hitherto unknown debts (e.g. Greece), extensions of blanket bailouts to banks (e.g. Ireland), reluctance to undertake adequate fiscal cuts, and moral suasion of the financial sector ("financial repression") to hold sovereign debt. In such cases, at least for reasonably large sovereigns, it may end up as incredible to not support the banks that are holding substantial quantities of sovereign debt. In turn, anticipation of this would allow the sovereign *ex ante* to continue building up of debt. Hence, the Eurozone may need another approach that breaks the sovereign-bank entanglement more directly:

4. An attractive proposal to achieve this has been provided by the Bruegel think tank. One interpretation of this proposal[2] is that a central debt management office in the Euro zone will decide how many 'blue' bonds can be issued by a sovereign, for instance, based on the ability of the office to match the sovereign's blue bond issuance against fiscal transfer from the sovereign to the office. The blue bonds *can* be held by banks; the idea is that these bonds are effectively collateralised and the issue of *ex-post* bailouts with resources other than those of the sovereign does not arise. However, if the sovereign wishes to borrow beyond the blue bond limit, then it must

---

2   See Delpla and Weizsacker 2010.

issue 'red' bonds. The red bonds *cannot* be held by banks, or in other words, they must be held by alternative investors such as hedge funds, pension funds, insurance companies, or more generally, those institutions that are not systemically important. This way, sovereign debt that is not effectively collateralised by tax receipts of the issuing sovereign can be credibly made to bear losses. In anticipation, the market for such debt would effectively discipline the sovereign from over-borrowing by reflecting its credit risk in bond yields and by doing so in a timely manner.

To summarise, banking union in Europe, as and when it is fully achieved, will likely manage the flow of credit risk emanating from weak banks to the balance sheet of their sovereigns. However, it is equally important to manage the flow of credit risk emanating from sovereigns to the banking system holding sovereign debt. To achieve the latter, some explicit steps need to be taken to ensure adequately risk-sensitive capital and liquidity treatment of risky sovereign debt, as well as to directly limit the ability of sovereigns to entangle banking system with their debt without advance collateralisation of such debt.

References

Acharya, V, I Drechsler and P Schnabl (2011), "A Pyrrhic Victory? Bank Bailouts and Sovereign Credit Risk", working paper, NYU-Stern.

Acharya, V and R Rajan (2011) "Sovereign Debt, Government Myopia and the Financial Sector", working paper, NYU-Stern.

Acharya, V and S Steffen (2012), "The Greatest Carry Trade Ever: Understanding Eurozone Bank Risks", working paper, NYU Stern.

Delpla, J and J Von Weizsacker (2010), "Eurobonds: The Blue Bond Concept and Its Implications", Bruegel Policy Brief, 2010/03, May.

Veron, N (2012), "Europe's Single Supervisory Mechanism and the Long Journey Towards Banking Union", Bruegel Policy Contribution, Issue 2012/16.

About the author

Viral V Acharya is the CV Starr Professor of Economics in the Department of Finance at New York University Stern School of Business (NYU-Stern). He is also the Program Director for Financial Economics and a Research Affiliate at the Centre for Economic Policy Research (CEPR); a member of Advisory Scientific Committee of European Systemic Risk Board (ESRB), Advisory Committee of Financial Sector Legislative Reforms Commission (FSLRC) of India, International Advisory Board of the Securities and Exchange Board of India (SEBI), and Advisory Council of the Bombay (Mumbai) Stock Exchange (BSE) Training Institute; and, an Academic Advisor to the Federal Reserve Banks of Chicago, Cleveland, New York and Philadelphia, and the Board of Governors. In addition, he is a Research Associate of the National Bureau of Economic Research (NBER) in Corporate Finance and Research Associate of the European Corporate Governance Institute (ECGI).

Viral's primary research interest is in theoretical and empirical analysis of systemic risk of the financial sector, its regulation and its genesis in government-induced distortions, an inquiry that cuts across several other strands of research – credit risk and liquidity risk, their interactions and agency-theoretic foundations, as well as their general equilibrium consequences. He has published articles in the *American Economic Review, Journal of Finance, Journal of Financial Economics, Review of Financial Studies, Journal of Business, Journal of Financial Intermediation, Rand Journal of Economics, Journal of Monetary Economics, Journal of Money, Credit and Banking*, and *Financial Analysts Journal*. He is a current editor of the *Journal of Financial Intermediation* (2009-) and associate editor of the *Journal of Finance* (2011-), *Review of Corporate Finance Studies* (RCFS, 2011-) and *Review of Finance* (2006-).

The Single European Market in Banking in decline – ECB to the rescue?

Daniel Gros
CEPS

The Eurozone is currently suffering from the affects of having an interdependent banking sector without a unified body to oversee it or to rescue it in times of crisis. This column argues that the current situation is unsustainable and that the ECB should assume these responsibilities for the sake of the Eurozone as a whole.

The prudential rules for banks are in principle the same throughout the EU, as they are codified by various EU directives and regulations. In reality, however, these supposedly common rules are implemented by national supervisors today in such a way as to 'balkanise' the Eurozone's banking markets.

These barriers impede the recycling of northern surpluses to the periphery, thus aggravating the crisis. This problem applies both to the rollover of the large accumulated stocks and the continuing flows of cross-border claims. The stocks result from the credit boom years up to 2007-8 during which enormous cross-border claims built up because banks were quite willing to recycle the current-account surpluses of the northern part of the Eurozone (i.e. Germany, Netherlands, Belgium and, effectively, Switzerland) which, cumulated over the last decade, amounted to almost €2,000 billion. The flow problem is that this area (of which Germany accounts for the biggest part) continues to run large current-account surpluses, which reflect a continuing excess supply of domestic savings (relative to domestic investment) of around €200 billion per annum.

Most of the northern excess savings have been (and continue to be) intermediated by regulated entities (predominantly banks, but also insurance companies). The regulatory and supervisory environment for these entities determines, to a large extent, how this surplus is invested, and therefore what part is available to finance the rollover of existing foreign debt and the continuing current-account deficits of the Eurozone periphery.

Interbank lending

An interesting case of how a tightening of regulation leads to unintended consequences is the application, since 2010, of the large exposure limits to interbank lending. This has *de facto* affected cross-border lending in particular, because before the crisis many cash-rich small banks in northern Europe were investing their surplus in southern Europe, usually via the only one partner they knew and trusted in each country. During a time when banks were considered safe it did not make sense for smaller banks (like the German Sparkassen) to distribute interbank risk over many partners. Moreover, until 2010 interbank lending (for up to three years) was exempted from the limit that the exposure to any one counterparty could not exceed 25% of capital (under the large exposure directive).

However, from the end of 2010 the large exposure limit is applied to interbank exposure as well. In practice this meant little for large institutions, but a lot for smaller ones. This change in the treatment of interbank lending might explain why interbank lending in general, and particularly across borders, continues to decline so much. This is a good example how a tightening of regulation during the bust is procyclical.

Moreover, supervision, i.e. the differential application and interpretation of common rules, can severely segment capital markets. National supervisors have to protect the interests of their home country, rather than the stability of the Eurozone's banking system. This implies that during times of financial stress they have an interest in keeping capital and liquidity within their home country – thus rendering the recycling of northern surpluses even more difficult.

Intra-group transfers

A priori one would think that at least within multinational banks funds can flow freely. This is not the case.

Many countries are at the same time host to subsidiaries and home country to large banks with subsidiaries abroad. In times of crisis, most supervisors, however, adopt an asymmetric attitude. They 'encourage' their home banks with subsidiaries abroad to repatriate as much capital and liquidity as possible, especially when the subsidiary is located in a country under financial stress. But at the same time, most supervisors also 'encourage' the subsidiaries of foreign banks on their home turf not to send any funds to their parent banks abroad, especially when they are located in countries with high-risk premia. Given that supervisors can easily make life miserable for any bank under their watch, this 'moral suasion' is usually effective.

This attitude of national supervisors is rational given that they typically have little direct information about foreign banks and given that it is their duty to protect the interests of their country, not that of the Eurozone as a whole.

The result of this 'ringfencing', as it is called, is gridlock, forcing the ECB to become the *de facto* clearer of the interbank market: for example the subsidiary of an Italian bank in Germany which is not allowed to transfer funds to its mother company in Italy will deposit its surplus fund at the Bundesbank. The Italian mother then will access the ECB's lending facilities to obtain the funding it needs. But the German supervisors are also pushing German banks with subsidiaries in Italy to source funding locally. This implies that even the Italian subsidiaries of German banks have to have recourse to financing from the ECB. The ECB thus has to substitute also the 'internal' capital market which was supposed to work within multinational banking groups. This is not only costly (as the ECB charges more for its borrowing than it pays for its deposits), but also leads to a generalised reduction in liquidity because the ECB requires collateral for all its lending.

Cross-border lending

This constitutes another area where differences in the attitude of national supervisors have an important impact.

The cross-border exposure of northern banks to the private sector in southern Europe is much larger than that to the public sector. It is here that existing regulation is increasing the cost of cross-border exposure given the ratings downgrades of the periphery. As a good example one can take the case of a country which is downgraded from AA to BBB (like Spain). Under the standardised approach the risk weight is only 20% for counterparties in AA-rated countries, but 100% for BBB-rated countries. A fall in the rating from AA to BBB therefore implies a jump of 80 percentage points in the risk weight. At a cost of capital of 25% this is equivalent to an increase in the effective cost of lending by two full percentage points. In practice this means a higher cost for cross-border lending, because Spanish supervisors are unlikely to apply this rule to domestic lending by Spanish banks whereas German supervisors are very likely to apply this rule to German banks lending to counterparts in Spain.

Conclusions

The main message is that the desire to protect the home turf in northern Europe has bottled up large amounts of savings there, thereby contributing to the severity of the Eurozone crisis. More generally, existing prudential rules have difficulties coping with a situation when country-specific macro-risk factors dominate individual idiosyncratic risk.

The creation of a 'single supervisory mechanism' headed by the ECB could have an important macroeconomic impact because the ECB would not penalise cross-border lending in the way national supervisors do today. The ECB would certainly not try to block intra-group transfers (provided that it was satisfied that the entire group was solvent). Moreover, the ECB would evaluate the risk weighting of cross border lending on the basis of the strength of the borrower, and not the rating of the country. A banking system supervised by the ECB would thus be able to provide again a mechanism to recycle excess northern savings into the Eurozone periphery.

About the author

Daniel Gros is the Director of the Centre for European Policy Studies (CEPS) in Brussels. He worked at the International Monetary Fund, in the European and Research Departments (1983-1986), then as an Economic Advisor to the Directorate General II of the European Commission (1988-1990). He has taught at the European College (Natolin) as well as at various universities across Europe, including the Catholic University of Leuven, the University of Frankfurt, the University of Basel, Bocconi University, the Kiel Institute of World Studies and the Central European University in Prague. His current research concentrates on the impact of the euro on capital and labour markets, as well as on the international role of the euro, especially in Central and Eastern Europe. He also monitors the transition towards market economies and the process of enlargement of the EU towards the east (he advised the Commission and a number of governments on these issues). He was advisor to the European Parliament from 1998 to 2005, and member of the *Conseil Economique de la Nation* (2003-2005); from 2001 to 2003, he was a member of the *Conseil d'Analyse Economique* (advisory bodies to the French Prime Minister and Finance Minister). Since 2002, he has been a member of the Shadow Council organised by *Handelsblatt*; and since April 2005, he has been President of San Paolo IMI Asset Management. He is editor of *Economie Internationale* and editor of *International Finance*. He has published widely in international academic and policy-oriented journals, and has authored numerous monographs and four books.

Two types of capital flight: Will a common deposit insurance help to stabilise the TARGET2 imbalances?

Frank Westermann
Osnabrueck University

With confidence in the Eurozone at an all time low, the problem of large-scale capital flight has come to the fore. This column argues that a common deposit insurance scheme as outlined in proposals for a banking union within the Eurozone would by itself not provide a solution to the problem.

A Friedman-type experiment helps a lot to illustrate the welfare implications of capital flight. Think of the owner of Spanish government bonds. Worried about default, she might want to leave the country and invest in safe assets abroad. Suppose she would put them in a backpack, take the train to Frankfurt and deposit her bonds in the safe. Then, there would be no welfare implications in either Germany or Spain. But the capital flight was also not successful from the investors' perspective. Upon arrival, she will still find government bonds in her backpack – and become aware that she cannot trade them into German Bunds in Frankfurt either without realising substantial losses.

Alternatively, the investor might give the government bonds to the central bank of Spain as collateral via the banking system, in return for fresh Euros that are "printed" electronically. These newly printed Euros can be wired via the TARGET2 system to Germany and deposited, say at Commerzbank in Frankfurt. This is more successful from the investors' perspective. She gets rid of Spanish bonds and can now buy German ones. However, in this case, the taxpayers in both countries are involved. As owners of the Eurosystem – the European system of central banks – they have just inherited the risk of default from the investor. The transaction generates a TARGET2-imbalance among central banks; a claim for Germany and a liability for Spain.[1]

A shift in deposits as a reason for TARGET2 imbalances?

In a recent Vox article, Paul De Grauwe analyses these TARGET2 balances, but from a different angle – the flight of deposits in the banking system. He thinks of a Spanish saver, who simply sends her deposits to Germany. This 'innocent' shift of deposits[2], he concludes, is of no concern for taxpayers. I will argue however, that this transaction is just the mirror image of the capital flight described above – and if it wasn't, it is not relevant to the TARGET2 debate. Deposit flight by itself is neither *necessary* nor *sufficient* for TARGET2 imbalances to occur.

To illustrate this point, compare two more complete scenarios. The Spanish resident sends her deposits to Germany *and* the Spanish private bank:

A. sells some of its assets in the market to cope with the withdrawal of deposits.

B. borrows money from the central bank of Spain to avoid such selling of assets.

Note that case (A) leaves TARGET2 balances among the central banks of Germany and Spain unchanged. Moving deposits to Germany does therefore not automatically lead to a TARGET2 imbalance. In equilibrium, the German private bank could for instance buy the assets that were sold by the Spanish bank, at market prices. This was the case before 2007, where neither a crisis, nor a TARGET2 real-time settlement system existed. And, it is still the case when moving deposits to other non-Eurozone countries.[3]

Only if the Spanish central bank gives credit to the private bank ('prints money') to *finance* this capital flight, there will be a TARGET imbalance among central banks.

---

1 See Garber (1998) and Sinn and Wollmershäuser (2011). Note that the owner of the Spanish government bond does not need to be a Spanish resident. They could be anywhere in the world, including Germany.
2 "While prudent, it is really just foreign exchange speculation…" (De Grauwe and Ji 2012)
3 Before the crisis there was of course also (C): the Spanish private bank borrows in the interbank market.

In this case, the assets of the Spanish private bank end up as collateral at the Bank of Spain, instead of being sold in the market.

The role of the national central banks

At the core of a welfare analysis must be the exchange between newly 'printed' money and non-marketable collateral-assets at the national central banks, and thus the second version of the Friedman-experiment above. The ECB has reduced collateral standards dramatically in the last years and has announced a 'full allotment' policy. De facto, it has performed the role as a lender of last resort to the private banks and thereby effectively insured deposits, as well as other bank liabilities.

Furthermore, the national central banks have assumed responsibility to assess the quality of collateral. Despite some haircuts[4], they still give out fresh money for balance sheet components that would not be of full value in the market. In this sense, the shifting of deposits becomes an indirect exchange of Spanish and German government bonds (or other types of risky and safe assets). It is facilitated by the central banks and would not be feasible in the market.

How is this different from expansionary monetary policies in other countries? As I have pointed out in a Vox article with Aaron Tornell, the TARGET2 system generates a common-pool – the Eurozone-wide demand for money. This allows the central bank of Spain to issue much more credit to its private banks, and accept much more non-marketable collateral, than it could have done if it was a country with its own currency. As a consequence, the central bank credit to private banks issued by Greece, Ireland, Italy, Portugal, and Spain have gone up by more than 1000% since the beginning of the

---

4   See Bindseil (2012). Note however, that the haircut only limits the maximum amount of money the banks can receive from the central bank. But it is not costly for them. If banks were to instead sell the asset in the market, they would immediately realise a loss. Borrowing from the central bank helps them to delay the realisation of losses. Furthermore, although haircuts are high at the margin, the average haircut is likely to be much lower. Finally, it is not clear whether the ECB could enforce its status as a senior lender in case of insolvency. On August 2nd, for instance, Mario Draghi declared that the ECB will "address private investors issues with creditor seniority" of the ECB in the context of the bond-purchase program.

crisis (See Figure 1).[5] It is a process that, we argue, leads to a classical tragedy-of-the-commons dilemma.[6]

Figure 1. Central banks' loans to credit institutions [billion €]

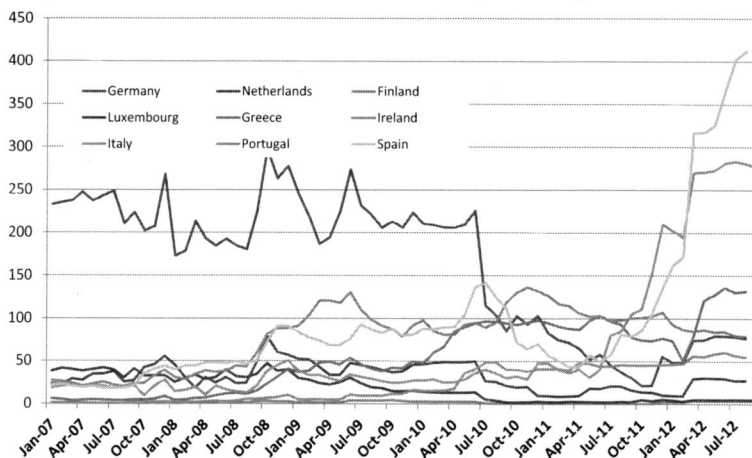

Source: Euro Crisis Monitor, Osnabrueck University.

Empirical relevance

Looking at the data helps to analyse which type of capital flight is more relevant for the European case – the deposit shifting or the flight from low-quality assets. We focus on Italy and Spain, where TARGET balances mounted rather recently, and De Grauwe and Ji suspect the balances are of no concern.

Figure 2 shows three time series for each country: central bank credit, private bank deposits, and TARGET2 balances. Each series starts at zero and displays the cumulative increment since 2007. First, looking at central bank credit and TARGET2 balances, one can see that they are nearly identical, with opposite signs. This confirms the argument above that deposit flight can only be relevant for TARGET2 balances if it is associated

---

5   Data on central bank credit and current TARGET2 balances are regularly updated on Osnabrueck's Euro-Crisis web-
    page: www.eurocrisismonitor.com
6   See Tornell (2012) for a formal analysis.

with a refinancing at the central bank. Furthermore, the red dashed lines show the patterns of deposits of households and firms (excluding government and MFI deposits).

In Spain, the decline in deposits starts just about the same time as the increase in TARGET2 balances, which is consistent with the conjecture of De Grauwe. But in magnitude, it is too small to explain the TARGET2 liability. Less than half of the over €400 billion TARGET2 liabilities could be explained by deposit flight.[7] Also, the current level of deposits is still clearly above the pre-2007 values. In Italy, the case is even clearer. Household deposits have not fallen at all. But nevertheless, Italy has accumulated more than €300b billion of TARGET2 liabilities within less than a year.

The empirical evidence thus supports the argument that deposit flight is not necessary to explain TARGET2 balances. The Italian case furthermore suggests that the Friedman-type of capital flight is present, even when no deposits are withdrawn and there is no remarkable change in the current account. It is not the existing deposits that leave, but those that were newly generated, after collateral rules were relaxed (8 December 2012) and banks borrowed from the central bank.

---

7   Even this decline in deposits may have nothing to do with the TARGET2 imbalance, as investors could also withdraw
    funds to spend within the country. Carstensen et al (2012) point out that an international deposit flight of private
    households would show up in the balance of payments. So far, however, there are only noticeable changes in the statistics
    for banks, not households.

Figure 2a. Private bank deposits, central bank credit and TARGET2 balances in Spain since 2007

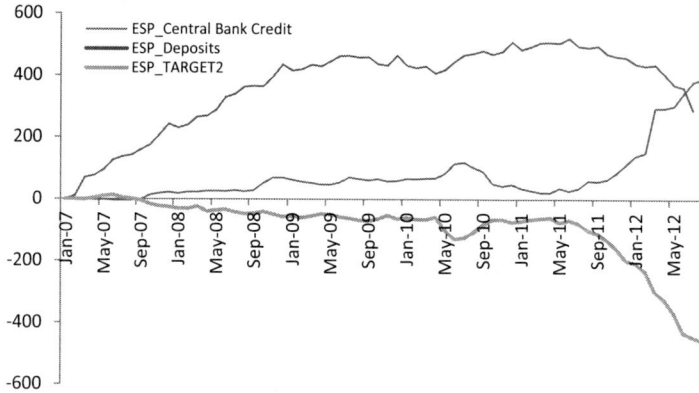

Figure 2b. Private bank deposits, central bank credit and TARGET2 balances in Italy since 2007

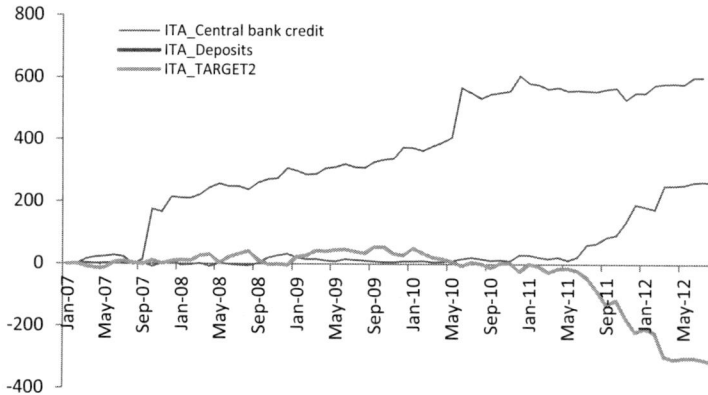

Note: The deposits exclude interbank credit and government deposits. 2007 is set to zero. The Graphs show the increment of each series since the beginning of the 2007/8 financial crisis.

Source: National central bank balance sheets and ECB.

Will deposit insurance help?

Large-scale deposit flight in Europe would be a serious problem. Most importantly, it would create an inefficient allocation of capital. It would also threaten to cause bank failures in the countries where the deposits leave. As shown above, however, the flight of deposits across borders is not the main source of capital flight and

TARGET2 imbalances so far.[8] A common deposit insurance in Europe that is currently debated, might stop the type of deposit flight that Paul De Grauwe has in mind. In this regard, it could indeed be a useful tool. But how about the other type of capital flight?

The main problem in Italy and Spain is the investors' apparent lack of confidence in government bonds and other assets of the aggregate banks' balance sheets. To address this problem, a common deposit insurance will not help. The only reason why the flight from government bonds might stop is that structural reforms make it likely that the countries can service their debts. It is also likely that banks need to write off losses on some other assets. If their equity base is not large enough, some of them will need to be closed or merged. The ECB on the other hand, should raise its collateral standards again. This would limit TARGET2 imbalances and capital flight via the Eurosystem of central banks. It is also needed to protect the interests of the taxpayers. Without these additional measures, however, even a full banking union might not stop the capital flight.

References

Bindseil, U (2012), "Deutschland und die Target2-Salden", *Frankfurter Allgemeine Zeitung*, 20 February.

Carstensen, K, W Nierhaus, T O Berg, B Born, C Breuer, T Buchen, S Elstner, C Grimme, S Henzel, N Hristov, M Kleemann, W Meister, J Plenk, A Wolf, T Wollmershäuser and P Zorn (2012), "ifo Konjunkturprognose 2012/2013: Erhöhte Unsicherheit dämpft deutsche Konjunktur erneut", *ifo Schnelldienst*, 65(13): 15-68

De Grauwe, P and Y Ji (2012), "What Germany should fear most is its own fear", VoxEU.org, 18 September.

---

8   See Schoenmaker and Gros (2012) and recent proposals of the EU commission.

Garber, P M (1999), "The target mechanism: Will it propagate or stifle a stage III crisis?", *Carnegie-Rochester Conference Series on Public Policy*, 51(1).

Sinn, H-W and T Wollmershäuser (2012), "Target Loans, Current Account Balances and Capital Flows: The ECB's Rescue Facility", *International Tax and Public Finance*, 19(4):468-508.

Schoenmaker, D and D Gros (2012), "A European Deposit Insurance and Resolution Fund", CEPS Policy Brief No. 283.

Tornell, A (2012), "The Dynamic Tragedy-of-the-Commons in the Eurozone, the ECB and Target2 Imbalances", UCLA, mimeo.

Tornell, A and F Westermann (2012), "The tragedy of the commons at the European Central Bank and the next rescue", VoxEU.org, 22 June.

About the author

Frank Westermann is Professor of International Economic Policy and Director of the Institute of Empirical Economic Research, at Osnabrueck University. Furthermore, he is Research Professor in the Division of Business Cycle Analyses and Surveys at the ifo Institute and Research Fellow at CESifo. Professor Westermann obtained his M.S. in Applied Economics in 1996 and his PhD in International Economics in 1998 at the University of California, Santa Cruz. He received his Habilitation and venia legendi in Economics from the University of Munich in 2004. The research interests of Frank Westermann include international economics, applied macroeconomics and economic policy. Jointly, with Aaron Tornell, he is author of *Boom-Bust Cycles and Financial Liberalization*, MIT Press 2005.

Banking union: The view from emerging Europe

Jeromin Zettelmeyer, Erik Berglöf and Ralph de Haas
European Bank for Reconstruction and Development (EBRD)

Although current banking union proposals are a critical step towards resolving the Eurozone crisis, they fall short of providing an integrated resolution and supervision framework for all of Europe. In addition, emerging European countries are concerned about insufficient influence on the proposed single supervisory mechanism and the prospect of fiscal responsibility for crises elsewhere. Some countries outside the Eurozone also worry that exclusion from potential access to the ESM might tilt the playing field against local banks. This chapter makes proposals for addressing these concerns.

A Eurozone-based 'banking union' could be crucial for the survival of the Eurozone and its future stability. It would help sever the much-feared 'death loop' between sovereigns that are exposed to losses in their national banking systems and banking systems directly and indirectly exposed to sovereigns. But would it also address the deficiencies of nationally based supervision and resolution of multinational banks which have plagued financially-integrated Europe for the last 15 years? Would it do so particularly from the perspective of emerging European countries, which depend on these cross-border banks much more than countries in western Europe do (Figure 1)? Or could it do more harm than good in this respect?

Authors' note: The views expressed in this chapter are the authors' only and do not necessarily represent those of the EBRD. The authors would like to thank, without implication, Bas Bakker, Katia D'Hulster, Achim Dübel, Christoph Klingen, Alexander Lehmann, Piroska Nagy, Lars Nyberg, Peter Tabak, Nicolas Veron and Beatrice Weder di Mauro for comments and suggestions on a longer version of this paper and Jonathan Lehne for excellent research assistance.

Figure 1. Asset share of foreign-owned banks in national banking systems

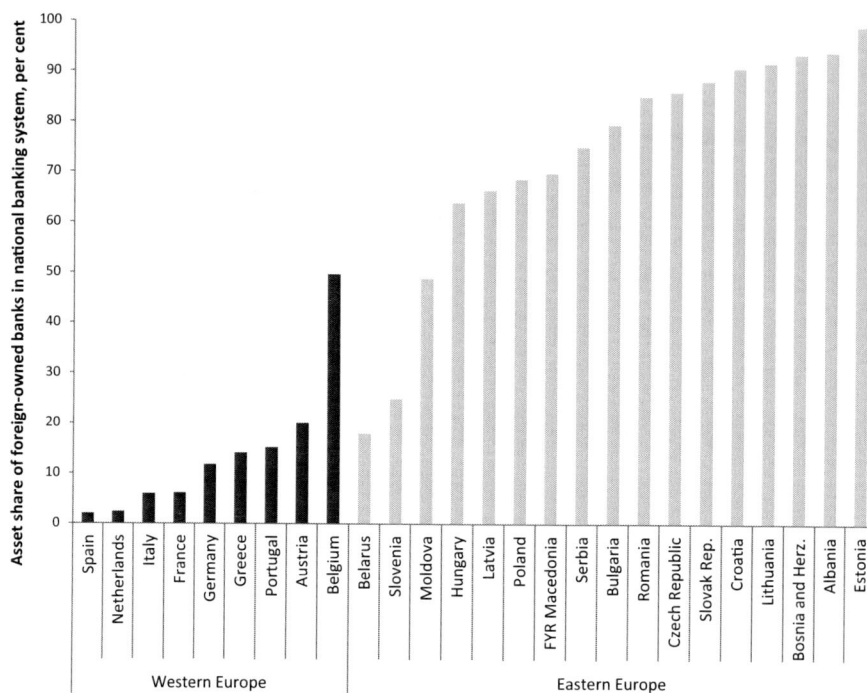

Source: Claessens and Van Horen (2012).

Tensions between actual and institutional financial integration in Europe

Multinational banks have been a force for financial development and economic growth, but they have also exacerbated credit booms, adding to the pain of crises – particularly in emerging Europe (See EBRD 2012 for a survey). Both the prevention and the mitigation of these crises has been complicated by poor coordination and conflicts of interest between the home and host countries of multinational banks. Three problems have stood out (For more details, see Allen et al. 2011, D'Hulster 2011 and EBRD 2012).

First, the presence of two supervisory authorities with diverging interests – in the home country of multinational groups and in the country hosting a subsidiary – can complicate effective oversight, and particularly macroprudential supervision. Home-country supervisors may have little incentive (and often no capacity) to police subsidiaries abroad unless they are 'systemic' from the perspective of the group (rather than from that of the host country). Host-country supervisors have this incentive, but may have little information about subsidiaries' parent banks. They will also find it more difficult to limit subsidiary lending than lending by standalone local banks, as they have little control over parent-bank funding, particularly with fixed-exchange-rate regimes. And even if they manage to exercise some control over subsidiary lending, this can be circumvented if multinational banks replace lending through their subsidiaries with cross-border lending directly from the parent or with lending through non-bank subsidiaries, such as leasing companies.

Second, cross-border banking can complicate crisis management. When problems come to light in either the home or host country, supervisors will generally have an incentive to either retrieve liquidity behind national borders or engage in ringfencing to prevent liquidity or assets from leaving the country. This may have negative externalities on the group as a whole, or parts of it, and give rise to further turmoil.

Lastly, home-host coordination is most difficult in the event of the failure of a multinational bank, resulting in a direct conflict of interest over how to share the fiscal burden of bank resolution. Indeed, it is the anticipation of such a situation that drives the diverging interests of home and host supervisors, both in normal times and during crisis management. In bank resolution the primary responsibility of national authorities is towards domestic taxpayers, ignoring cross-border externalities (for example, if rescuing the parent bank helps the subsidiary, and vice versa). As a result, too little capital is likely to be invested in a failing multinational bank. This may make it difficult to maximise the bank's value as a going concern, and induce outcomes that are both inefficient and detrimental for systemic stability – such as a breakup and separate nationalisation when the bank would have more value, in a future reprivatisation, as a single entity (See Freixas 2003 and Goodhart and Schoenmaker 2009).[1]

Even before the banking union idea gained momentum during 2012, the EU introduced several reforms that were designed to address this problem. Since 2011, coordination failures and disagreements between national banking authorities in the EU can, in principle, be tackled by the European Banking Authority, the EU-level body charged with coordinating and, if necessary, arbitrating between banking supervisors. However, as market pressures on the home countries of several Eurozone banks have intensified with the widening crisis in the single-currency area, some home and host authorities of these banks have undertaken a series of unilateral and seemingly ring-fencing measures, presumably reflecting the fact that the responsibility for resolution, and ultimate fiscal losses, remains national (See EBRD 2012, Box 3.4.). Partly in response to these developments, the 'Vienna Initiative' – an informal cross-border coordination group created at the height of the 2008-9 crisis and involving international financial institutions, home and host country authorities, and representatives of the major multinational banks – has recently been revived.[2]

A recent legislative proposal by the European Commission (EU framework for bank recovery and resolution, June 2012) proposes to address some of these problems by creating 'resolution colleges', analogous to the supervisory colleges chaired by the European Banking Authority, and giving it a mediation role between the national authorities sitting on these colleges. However, the European Banking Authority's scope for resolving conflicts of interest in this area would remain constrained by Article 38 of its regulation, which compels it to "ensure that no decision adopted pursuant to [settlement of disagreements between national authorities in cross-border situations] impinges in any way on the fiscal responsibilities of Member States." This means that it

1 The fragmentation of the financial conglomerate Fortis, systematically important in Belgium, the Netherlands and Luxembourg, is an example of how limited supervisory cooperation during an acute crisis may result in suboptimal outcomes.
2 The Vienna Initiative 2.0 was launched in the Spring of 2012 and adopted a set of guiding principles for home-host coordination.

will not be able to take a decision on a bank resolution issue that determines how fiscal losses are distributed across countries – which, unfortunately, is likely to be the main source of disagreement among national authorities.

Making an Eurozone banking union attractive

By creating an institutional structure that matches the actual perimeter of Europe's integrated banking system as closely as possible, a European banking union could close these institutional gaps and deal with the home host problem once and for all (at least as far as Europe is concerned). Indeed, this is what several recent proposals aim to achieve, in addition to 'saving' the Eurozone.[3] The question is whether the official proposal that is currently on the table – creating an ECB led single supervisory mechanism that would unlock the possibility of direct recapitalisation of euro area banks from ESM resources – meets this standard.[4]

The answer is clearly "no". Since resolution authority would remain at the national level in the foreseeable future, the proposal would not address coordination problems in the area of resolution, which are likely to spill over to crisis management. Nor would it address supervisory coordination failures with respect to multinational banks for which either the parent or a subsidiary is located outside the area covered by the single supervisory mechanism. In addition, two concerns about the proposal have recently been articulated by emerging European countries are either in the Eurozone or see themselves as future members.

- One worry is that the ECB might devote less attention to the supervision of a small country's financial system than a national supervisor. This could happen if the ECB were to focus supervision on large groups (essentially displaying the bias that has

---

3 See Allen et al (2011), Fonteyne et al (2010), Hellwig et al (2012), Pisany-Ferry et al (2012) and Schoenmaker and Gros (2012).

4 See Euro area summit statement, 28 June 2012, and "Proposal for a council regulation conferring specific tasks on the European Central Bank concerning policies relating to the prudential supervision of credit institutions." See *http://ec.europa.eu/internal_market/finances/docs/committees/reform/20120912-com-2012-511_en.pdf*

been attributed to home country authorities) at the expense of preventing local banking crises which are unlikely to pose a systemic threat to Europe as a whole. Note that there is nothing in the commission's proposal that would directly give rise to such a bias, as the ECB would have explicit supervisory responsibility for individual financial institutions – including subsidiaries. However, there is scepticism on the side of some countries whether the ECB would have sufficient incentives to focus on the local as well as the union-wide systemic level.

- Another concern is that the banking union would give rise to moral hazard, as it would combine a common fiscal backstop (a direct recapitalisation instrument housed with the European Stability Mechanism, as envisaged by the European Council in late June) with national resolution authority. A national resolution authority may not be as robust in, for example, imposing losses on creditors of failing banks as they would be if fiscal losses were borne at the national level. Furthermore, national authorities would also retain other policy instruments (for example, the power to tax and subsidise, and housing policies) which influence the likelihood and fiscal costs of banking crises even in the presence of a very powerful and competent joint supervisor.

Assuming that it is not possible to go for the first-best governance structure in one step – an integrated supervision, resolution, deposit insurance and fiscal backstop at the EU level – the European Commission's proposal could be complemented as follows to address these concerns.

First, remaining coordination gaps could be mitigated by the creation of one or several cross-border stability groups for emerging Europe, following the example of the Baltic-Nordic Stability Group (see EBRD 2012, box 3.5). Membership would include host country authorities, the ECB, the European Banking Authority, the European Commission, the European Financial Committee (representing the European council), and home country authorities (particularly ministries of finance, but also non-Eurozone supervisory authorities).[5] In addition to improving supervisory coordination, these could mitigate coordination problems in a crisis by undertaking crisis management exercises and agreeing ahead of time on how resolution cases would be approached. They would also create a link between resolution authorities and the ECB.

Second, the supervisory function within the ECB should be structured in a way that gives smaller members of the single supervisory mechanism sufficient voice. For example, in addition to a board that takes the main decisions, the supervisory function could be governed by a larger 'Prudential Council' that would include representatives of national supervisors, which would exercise oversight over the actions of the executive board (see Véron 2012).

Third, national authorities of member countries could be given the option to impose certain macroprudential instruments, such as additional prudential capital buffers, on subsidiaries and domestic banks. These may be justified, for example, to deal with more volatile credit cycles in emerging European countries, or to offset higher macroeconomic and financial vulnerabilities. The ECB could set minimum buffers and retain a veto over national decisions which are deemed to run counter to system-wide stability.

Lastly, there should be an *ex ante* fiscal burden-sharing agreement between national fiscal authorities and the Eurozone fiscal backstop that forces the national level to take some fiscal losses if (or indeed before) they are taken at the European level. In other words, the European Stability Mechanism should not primarily cover 'first losses' passed on to the taxpayer, but only 'catastrophic losses', once the national fiscal burden exceeds a predetermined level (for example, 20 percentage points of GDP).

---

5 In practice, this could be one group in which most business is conducted by smaller committees focused on specific host countries; or possibly three groups focused on emerging European countries in the Eurozone, the non-Eurozone EU, and the EU neighbourhood, respectively.

Bringing in the 'outs'

By staving off financial chaos in Europe, the banking union would benefit even emerging European countries that are not members of the Eurozone. At the same time, there is a concern among some of these countries that a common fiscal backstop for the Eurozone banking system may tilt the competitive balance against banks which are headquartered outside the single currency area. Although foreign subsidiaries would not be eligible for direct support, they might be expected to benefit indirectly through their parent banks, making it harder for domestically owned institutions outside the Eurozone to compete. A further concern, already mentioned above, is that home-host coordination problems will persist after the creation of the single supervisory mechanism. Non-EU countries could not join the mechanism, and although non-Eurozone EU members could opt in, they are unlikely to do so, since they would be excluded from the possibility of direct recapitalisation by the ESM, and may not want to lose supervisory control. From the perspective of these "outs", Eurozone home authorities would simply be replaced by one powerful eurozone home supervisor – the ECB.

One obvious remedy for EU countries that see net benefits from banking union membership would of course be to join the Eurozone. However, many of these countries may not yet meet the macroeconomic criteria required for accession, or may wish to retain autonomous monetary policy for some time. For these reasons, it is worth exploring whether the benefits of banking union membership could be extended to non-Eurozone countries in full or in part. Several options are conceivable, none of them simple:

First, the European Stability Mechanism treaty could be modified to allow non-Eurozone members to join join if they also join the single supervisory mechanism – that is, to become full members of the banking union without necessarily adopting the single currency. In addition to access to the European Stability Mechanism, these countries should also be allowed access to euro liquidity (through swap lines with the ECB, see below). The fact that these countries continue to have their own monetary policy and hence an extra instrument to influence credit growth could be addressed by letting national authorities absorb most of the 'first loss' should anything go wrong in their banking sectors.

Second, it may be possible to create an 'associate member' status in the banking union for non-Eurozone countries. Unlike their Eurozone counterparts, they would not give up supervisory control, nor would they benefit from the European Stability Mechanism. However, the ECB could give them access to euro liquidity – in the form of foreign-exchange swap lines against domestic collateral. In return, national supervisors would agree to share information with the ECB and to a periodic review of their supervisory policies. Swap lines would be committed from one review period to the next, and rolled over subject to the satisfactory completion of the review.

Third, it might be possible to devise a supervisory regime that allows the host country to retain significant supervisory control but at the same time mitigates the coordination problem in respect of multinational banking groups. As described above, although host countries have formal supervisory power over subsidiaries, they have sometimes had limited de facto control because of a lack of information about, and influence over, parent bank funding. One way of mitigating this problem would be to have the ECB share supervisory responsibility for the subsidiaries of multilateral groups in return for giving host supervisors information about, and some influence over, the supervision of the group. The latter could range from normal participation in the single supervisory mechanism (with respect to the group) to the right to be heard.

The first of these options would (at best) apply to EU members only. However, there would seem to be no legal or conceptual reason why the second or third avenues could not also apply to European countries that are not (or not yet) members of the EU.

Conclusion

Recent proposals to unify bank supervision, harmonise resolution frameworks and transform the ESM into a fiscal safety net for banking systems in the Eurozone could go a long way toward arresting the present crisis and addressing coordination failures between home – and host-country authorities within the single currency area. At the same time, they raise concerns particularly among emerging European countries. Potential members worry that the proposed single supervisory mechanism might pay insufficient attention to the stability of national banking systems, and are concerned that banking union membership might lead to fiscal liabilities caused by poor policies elsewhere. At the same time, countries outside the Eurozone fear that domestic banks may lose ground against their Eurozone-based competitors that will have potential access to recapitalisation from ESM resources.

While these concerns need to be taken seriously, they can be overcome. A move towards supranational resolution mechanisms remains essential over the medium term, but if it cannot be achieved in the short term, the proposal could be improved with other means. Moral hazard could be addressed through an *ex ante* rule requiring countries receiving ESM fiscal support to share banking-related fiscal losses up to a pre-determined level. Coordination gaps can be reduced by cross-border 'stability groups' that include home and host country authorities, the ECB and the EBA. Lastly, non-Eurozone countries should be allowed to opt into the ESM if they also join the single supervisory mechanism. Apart from full membership, intermediate options could also be considered which would extend some but not all benefits and obligations of membership to all financially integrated European countries – including countries outside the EU.

References

Allen, F, T Beck, E Carletti, P R Lane, D Schoenmaker and W Wagner (2011) Cross-border banking in Europe: implications for financial stability and macroeconomic policies, Centre for Economic Policy Research, London.

Claessens, S and N Van Horen (2012), "Foreign banks: trends, impact and financial stability", IMF Working Paper No. 12/10, Washington, D.C.

D'Hulster, K (2011) "Incentive conflicts in supervisory information sharing between home and host supervisors", World Bank Policy Research Working Paper No. 5871, Washington, D.C.

EBRD (2012), *Transition Report*, London.

Fonteyne, W, W Bossu, L Cortavarria-Checkley, A Giustiniani, A Gullo, D Hardy, and S Kerr (2010) "Crisis management and resolution for a European banking system", IMF Working Paper No. 10/70, Washington, D.C.

Freixas, X (2003) "Crisis management in Europe", eds. J. Kremers, D. Schoenmaker and P. Wierts, *Financial Supervision in Europe*, Cheltenham: Edward Elgar, pp. 102-19.

Goodhart, C and D Schoenmaker (2009) "Fiscal burden sharing in cross-border banking crises", *International Journal of Central Banking*, Vol. 5, pp. 141–65.

Hellwig, M, A Sapir, M Pagano, V Acharya, L Balcerowicz, A Boot, M K Brunnermeier, C Buch, I van den Burg, C Calomiris, D Focarelli, A Giovannini, D Gros, A Ittner, D Schoenmaker, and C Wyplosz (2012) "Forbearance, Resolution and Deposit Insurance", *ESRB Reports of the Advisory Scientific Committee* No. 1/July 2012, Frankfurt.

Pisani-Ferry, J, A Sapir, N Vernon and G Wolff (2012) "What kind of European banking union?", issue 2012/12, June 2012, Bruegel Institute.

Schoenmaker, D and D Gros (2012) "A European deposit insurance and resolution fund", Centre for European Policy Studies Working Document No. 364, Brussels.

Véron, N (2012), "Europe's Single Supervisory Mechanism and the Long Journey towards Banking Union", Briefing paper for the ECON Committee (Economic and Monetary Affairs) of the European Parliament, October.

About the authors

Jeromin Zettelmeyer is Deputy Chief Economist and Director of Research of EBRD, which he joined in 2008 after 14 years at the International Monetary Fund. His research interests include financial crises, sovereign debt, economic growth and transition economies. He is the author of *Debt Defaults and Lessons from a Decade of Crises* (with Federico Sturzenegger, MIT press, 2007), and was the lead editor of the last three EBRD Transition Reports. He is Vice-Chair of the World Economic Forum's Global Agenda Council on Fiscal Sustainability, and a Fellow of the Centre for Economic Policy Research (CEPR).

Erik Berglöf joined the EBRD as the Chief Economist in January 2006. The Office of the Chief Economist provides the economic and political analysis that underpins the EBRD's investment decisions and guides the Bank's strategic planning. He was formerly Director of the Stockholm Institute of Transition Economics (SITE) at the Stockholm School. He is a Research Fellow of CEPR and the William Davidson Institute at the University of Michigan. He was previously assistant professor at ECARES, Université Libre de Bruxelles and has held visiting positions at Stanford University.

He has written extensively on financial contracting and corporate governance. In particular, he has applied theoretical insights to the study of differences between financial systems, and specific ownership and control arrangements. More recently, his work has focused on bankruptcy.

He has also been involved in several capacity-building initiatives in transition countries, including as Director of the Center for Economics and Financial Research (CEFIR) in Moscow and the Baltic International Center for Economic Policy Studies (BICEPS) in Riga. He has served as special adviser to the Prime Minister of Sweden and on several government commissions and EU-related panels. In addition, he has been a consultant to the World Bank and the IMF.

Ralph de Haas is Deputy Director of Research at the EBRD. His main research interests include international banking, microfinance, and development economics. He is currently working on randomised field experiments measuring the impact of microfinance on poverty alleviation in Mongolia, Morocco, and Bosnia. Other research projects deal with internal capital markets in multinational banks, the effects of the global credit crunch on international bank lending, and the impact of foreign bank entry on small business finance.

He has published or has papers forthcoming in the *Review of Financial Studies*, *Journal of Financial Intermediation*, *American Economic Review Papers and Proceedings*, *Economic Policy*, *Journal of Banking & Finance*, *Economics of Transition*, and *Financial Markets, Institutions and Instruments*, among other journals.

Five lessons from the Spanish cajas debacle for a new euro-wide supervisor

Luis Garicano
London School of Economics

Economists in the Eurozone seem set on the principle of a single supervisory body to make up a part of a new banking union. This column argues that when thinking about the inner workings of this new institution, we need to learn from the mistakes of the Spanish regulators in dealing with the cajas.

For a financial crisis of such a magnitude that it threatens both the solvency of the Spanish state and effectively destroyed the credibility of the Spanish supervisors, it is surprising how slowly it has developed. With a similar combination of a large real estate bubble and a complicated financial crisis the Irish bank recapitalisation (and the nationalisation of Anglo Irish) in January 2009 took place a full three years before the entire Spanish financial system had to confront the reality of its losses with the collapse of Bankia in May 2012.[1] By this time, the Eurozone crisis was in full swing, and Spain did not have access to the markets, forcing Spain to seek European help. This would have been unnecessary had the crisis been forced in the open before the euro doubts came to the fore and while Spain had a low debt to GDP ratio and easy access to the market. An additional casualty of the crisis, apart from Spain's solvency, was the Banco de España's reputation, as evidenced by the fact that Europe forced Spain to have an external private sector firm (Oliver Wyman) undertake the stress tests.

Why was the crisis response so slow? What can we learn from the Spanish supervisory debacle for the future European Single Supervisory Mechanism?

---

1 To be sure, Irish banks (particularly Anglo Irish) unlike the Spanish *cajas*, were exposed to the US real estate bubble as well, and have been able to generate lower pre-provisioning profits than the Spanish financial system. This, however, does not justify the length of the delay.

A hint of the answer comes from the knowledge that, with a few relatively small exceptions, the Spanish financial crisis has been a crisis of the *caja* (savings and loan) sector. Adding up the previous injections by the Spanish bank rescue funds (FROB) to the estimates of the recent official Oliver Wyman (September 2012) report, just the three most problematic Spanish *cajas* (Bankia, CatalunyaCaixa and Novagalicia) have had capital deficits (to be covered partly or fully by the taxpayer) of €54 billion – over 5% of Spanish GDP, a larger amount than what Spain will have to request from the European rescue funds.

The Oliver Wyman report, the fourth evaluation of the solvency of the financial system in three years, makes very clear that the problematic *cajas* were busy reclassifying, refinancing, and extending loans to cover up their losses in the previous four years. Indeed, the evidence of a cover up on the part of the worst *cajas'* management during 2008, 2009, and 2010 was overwhelming.[2] And yet, the Banco de España did not confront it.

In fact, it kept being surprised when in each *caja* that failed the holes uncovered where larger than expected. Already the first entity that was intervened (CCM) as far back as March 2009, showed that the real NPL levels post intervention (17.6%) were more than twice as large as the reported ones. This should have been the point for the Banco de España to get ahead of the curve by ordering an audit of the whole sector (which eventually did happen, three and a half years later). Instead, no one went back to the other *cajas* to try to correct the numbers. Each further intervention (CajaSur, CAM) resulted in similar jumps, and each time the reaction was circumscribed to the fallen entity. More evidence of a cover up was uncovered, in a widely reported analysis, by Santiago López Díaz from Credit Suisse. He showed (Coterill 2010) that there was a clear cyclical pattern in non performing loan (NPL) recognition: NPLs increased sharply in the first two months of each quarter, and then became systematically negative in the third one, in the third one, when the numbers had to be reported. Finally, all

---

2   For a view at the time, see Cuñat and Garicano (2009a).

market observers were shocked that the stock of real estate developer loans (32% of Spain's GDP) was still growing through that period (see Figure 1), in spite of large bankruptcies in the sector and few new developments being started. This suggests many loans were being informally restructured or refinanced.

Figure 1 The fast buildup and slow drop-off of real estate developer loans (€bn)

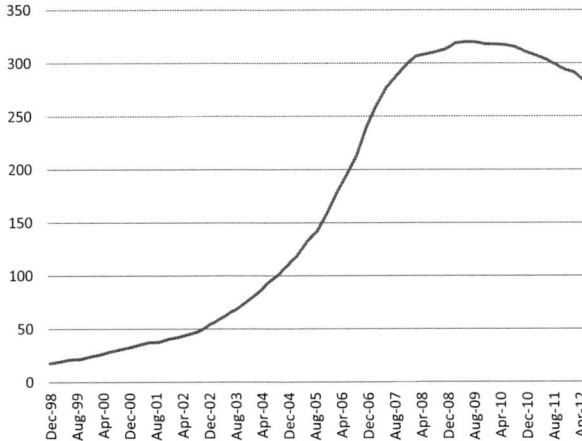

Source: Banco de España. Series BE_4_19.10.

If the evidence was in plain sight, why did the Banco de España not react? There is no intimation by anyone of outright corruption in the Banco de España supervisory role, and given the professionalism of the institution it is unlikely that there was any. There are four likely reasons for this failure and they suggest lessons for other supervisors.

All supervisors are reluctant to uncover their own previous mistakes – an instance of career concerns (i.e. jamming the signals to improve the perception of performance, as in Holmstrom 1982) of those responsible for the failure. Thus not surprisingly, Banco de España supervisors had little interest in discovering that Spain's vaunted regulator had in fact missed the largest financial crisis in the history of the country. Unfortunately, often supervisors in charge of the failing entity in the years of the debt run up were the ones charged with uncovering the problems. Indeed, they were not too eager to put in question their own previous work.

But all supervisors have career concerns, and they would not have mattered as much had the crisis developed more suddenly. The dynamics were partly dulled by the existence of dynamic provisions, which were in that sense working as desired. Spain was the leader in the introduction of a dynamic provision – a provisioning tool that forces banks to increase provisions without reference to any specific loan. The intention of this tool was twofold: to mitigate the bad times, and to cool the booms in the good times (Holmstrom and Tirole 1997). Dynamic provisions were endorsed as part of the Basel III standards in December 2010, in part on the strength of Spain's experience. And indeed the existing evidence (Jiménez et al. 2012) shows that the tool worked as intended, dampening the credit boom and softening somewhat the credit crunch. However, it is clear by now that their level was not nearly enough, as their size – 3% of GDP at their highest point (2004) – was simply not of a magnitude commensurate with the credit losses.

A more insidious consequence of the existence of this buffer is that it allowed the reality to be hidden in plain sight for longer than it would have been otherwise possible. Without the provisions, the reality of the *caja*'s accounts would have become much faster a concern, and would have imposed itself on the regulator. While this is not an argument to abandon dynamic provisions, it is an argument to make sure to take into account the impact they may have in dulling supervisor´s incentives.

Another reason for the lack of action by the Banco de España was the lack of an appropriate resolution framework at the time. Had the Banco de España ordered an audit of the system after uncovering numerous irregularities in CCM, it would have not been able to deal with the capital shortfalls uncovered as there was no appropriate resolution regime in Spain at the time (indeed there has not been one until the Summer of 2012).

But the main explanation for the supervisory failure of the Banco de España has to do with the political control of the *cajas*. As in many previous financial crises (most recently, the Savings and Loans in the USA, the Asian crisis and the current Irish crisis), governance played a critical role in the development of the Spanish crisis. In the Spanish case, the supervisor, confronted with powerful and well connected ex-politicians decided to look the other way in the face of obvious building trouble.

Indeed the political connection of the managers of the entities was a good predictor of brewing trouble. Anecdotally, the worst in terms of the losses it will impose on taxpayers, Caja Madrid/Bankia, was the most politicised. For just one nugget, the appointment of the CEO that led it in its out-of-control-bubble years was the result of a formal but secret pact between the Madrid conservative Popular Party and the main hard left trade union in 1986, CCOO, which involved among other things access by the union to the executive commission and participation in restructuring decisions behind the back of the *caja* board. More systematic evidence of the role played by these governance issues is provided in a 2009 paper (Cuñat and Garicano 2009b) where we showed that *cajas* with chief executives who had no previous banking experience (!), no graduate education, and were politically connected did substantially worse in the run up to the crisis (granting more real estate developer loan, up to half of the entire loan book in some instances) and during the crisis (with higher NPLs).

Even more important was the role of these political connections in diluting the role of the supervisor after the crisis started, in what was meant to be the crisis resolution stage but which was in fact a crisis cover up stage. The mergers that were decided followed political and regional criteria, rather than economic rationales. The Popular Party *cajas* (those controlled by Popular Party regional politicians) merged together, which meant that two of the most problematic *cajas* in the crisis (Bancaja from Valencia and Caja Madrid) ended up as part of the same undercapitalised (now nationalised) entity. The two Galician *cajas* also merged, because Galicia "must have" a local credit institution, creating a monster that is also nationalised. Same with the medium-sized Catalan *cajas*, also now nationalised. In all of these instances, the regulator was mindful of the figures, and understood the costs of these politicised entities, but refused to impose its will in the face of concerted actions by the politicians.

What are the takeaways of the Spanish supervisory debacle for the new European supervisor? I would suggest five.

First, in systemic crisis, the problems do not necessarily have to affect large institutions, but may instead impact a lot of small institutions. Moreover, the small institutions may play the role of the canary in the mine in anticipating the systemic problems. The supervisor should have all the relevant information and that requires covering (essentially) the entire banking system, as in the European Commission 12 of September SSM proposal (COM 2012 511).

Second, career concerns of supervisors are crucial. Like auditors post Enron, supervisors must be rotated from accounts with a certain frequency, and certainly when problems are building up in the system.

Third, dynamic provisioning is a good idea, but the supervisor must be mindful it may delay decision making in problem cases and as a result, and contrary to their intent, make the crisis larger than it should have otherwise been.

Fourth, the supervisor must be able and willing to stand up to politicians. Tackling corporate governance issues in semi-public entities is delicate, as it involves challenging regional power centres, political parties and unions. However, the supervisor must have the courage to be as intrusive as necessary to ensure the necessary professionalism and knowledge in these institutions in the good times, even in the absence of obvious problems, in the knowledge that when they fall, they are likely to take the taxpayers money with them.

Fifth, supervision and an appropriately tough resolution regime must go hand in hand. It is impossible for the supervisor to act sufficiently aggressively to build confidence and get in front of the market if there is no appropriate resolution regime that it can use once irregularities and capital shortfalls are uncovered in the supervised entities.

References

Coterill, J (2010), 'What is up with Spanish mortgage lending?', FT Alphaville, Jul 20.

Cuñat, V and L Garicano (2009a), '¿Para cuándo la reestructuración del sistema financiero español?', El Pais, September 13.

Cuñat, V and L Garicano (2009b), 'Did Good Cajas Extend Bad Loans? The Role of Governance and Human Capital in Cajas' Portfolio Decisions', FEDEA monograph.

Holmstrom, B (1982/99), 'Managerial incentive problems: A dynamic perspective', *Review of Economic Studies* 66, 169–182; originally published in Essays in Economics and Management in Honour of Lars Wahlbeck, Helsinki, Finland.

Holmstrom, B and J Tirole (1997), 'Financial Intermediation, Loanable Funds, and the Real Sector', The Quarterly Journal of Economics 112(3), 663-691.

Jiménez, G, S Ongena, J L Peydró and J Saurina (2012), 'Macroprudential Policy, Countercyclical Bank Capital Buffers and Credit Supply: Evidence from the Spanish Dynamic Provisioning Experiments', Banco de España. Mimeo.

About the author

Luis Garicano is a Professor of Economics and Strategy, Departments of Management and of Economics, and a Research Fellow with the Productivity and Innovation Programme at the Centre for Economic Performance (CEP), at the London School of Economics. He is also a Research Fellow at the Centre for Economic Policy Research (CEPR), London; and Director, Catedra Fedea-McKinsey.

Professor Garicano received his PhD in Economics from the University of Chicago in June 1998, and was assistant, associate and full professor at the Booth School of Business of the University of Chicago between 1998 and 2008. His research interests focus on the interaction between the governance of firms and other institutions and the economy as a whole. In particular he has studied, theoretically and empirically, how the organisation of firms affects economy-wide aggregates such as economic growth, productivity and wage inequality, or how the governance of banks and of the financial system affect economic outcomes; and, conversely, how economy wide changes such as advances in information technology or changes in regulation affect the use of incentives and the internal structure of firms. His research has been published in the top journals in economics including the *American Economic Review*, the *Journal of Political Economy*, and the *Quarterly Journal of Economics* and earned him the Banco Herrero Prize for the best Spanish researcher under 40 in the fields of economics, business and social research.

A first step towards a banking union

Vasso Ioannidou
Tilburg University

On 12 September the European Commission unveiled its proposals for the transfer of supervisory responsibilities to a European level to the ECB. This is the first step towards a banking union, with the transfer of deposit insurance and resolution at a European level being the other two. This column reviews the main advantages of moving supervision to a European level and to the ECB in particular and highlights some of the resulting challenges and risks, also in relation to the other two steps as the three functions – supervision, deposit insurance, and resolution – are intimately interconnected.

The European Commission's proposal in brief

The European Commission's proposal suggests that all banks in the Eurozone are subject to prudential supervision by the ECB as of January 2014 (European Commission 2012a). The supervision of large and systemically important banks and banks that are under government support should be phased in a year earlier; although this seems to be overly optimistic on the speed with which agreement on 'fine tuning' the proposal can be reached. EU countries that have not adopted the euro can choose to be supervised by the ECB on a voluntary basis. In a separate proposal (EC2012b), the Commission also suggests that the European Banking Authority (EBA) should not only remain in charge of creating a single 'rulebook', but that is also tasked with the creation of uniform supervisory practices – a single 'supervisory handbook' – to ensure that uniform rules and enforcement apply for all EU banks as to create and maintain a level playing field.

As it stands currently, the Commission's proposal gives sweeping powers to the ECB for all aspects of bank supervision as well as some crisis management powers. Within the Eurozone, the ECB will be responsible for licensing credit institutions, ongoing bank supervision to ensure compliance with safety and soundness, early intervention in troubled institutions with powers to require corrective measures such as capital and liquidity injections, and improvements in corporate governance. The ECB will also have the power, "in cooperation with the relevant resolution authorities", to close down an institution if necessary. Currently the resolution of failed institutions rests with national authorities. As part of the banking union, this task is expected to move to a European level to increase the speed with which failed institutions are wound up, internalise externalities that arise in the case of cross-border institutions, and reduce regulatory capture. The identity, structure, and the exact division of tasks between the ECB and the resolution authority are still to be delineated, but one thing is known for sure: this decision will have important implications for the ultimate success of this first step. The way institutions die determines how they live! Beyond any corrective behavior that any policeman can hope to achieve, the way the courts will handle the case is likely to have a first order effect in creating the right incentives *ex ante*.

What does moving supervision to a European level buy? And what does it cost?

Moving supervision to a European level does not necessarily imply that supervision should be moved to the ECB. That is a separate issue – one that is addressed below. Before turning to that, however, it is important to understand what moving supervision to a European level buys and what it costs.

Having a single European supervisor should increase the likelihood that the rules and enforcement that govern the regulation and supervision of banks would be more uniform across the various EU or Eurozone countries, creating a level playing field in an integrated financial market, ensuring minimum standards, and reducing risk-shifting opportunities abroad (see, for example, Ongena et al, forthcoming). Uniform rules and enforcement is also a minimum prerequisite for deposit insurance and resolution to be moved to a European level without causing social and political upheaval as both will be pre-funded by bank and state contributions from all participating countries. Moving supervision to a European level will also increase the distance of supervisors from powerful national lobbies, reducing the scope for regulatory forbearance. As the financial crisis highlighted, there is a tendency by national supervisors to side with their troubled banks in hiding information from the public and other supervisors, delaying the recognition of losses, postponing corrective measures, and resulting in larger eventual losses. The lack of sufficient independence of some national supervisors from the executive (in combination with insufficient and explicit powers to intervene) magnifies this problem. This problem is also at the heart of the current vicious cycle between bank and sovereign risk. Finally, having a single European supervisor will help improve the oversight of cross-border institutions and perhaps more importantly, also allow for an earlier detection of systemic risk at the level of the EU as a whole.

But what are the costs? Creating a new pan-European supervisor 'from scratch' is a daunting task and a very expensive one too, especially given the EU's current state of fiscal finances. The infrastructure that needs to be put in place and the highly skilled employees that will need to be hired in such a short period of time should not be taken lightly. (Talent and skills are scarce, especially when the other side of the camp pays multiple times more.) And what are we supposed to do with the current infrastructure and employees at the national competent authorities (some of whom have 'jobs for life')? Moving supervision at the European level does not require that we 'reinvent the wheel'. The new European supervisor could rely on the national supervisors for the day-to-day supervision, especially for the smaller and less systemically important institutions where a deep knowledge of the local economies may be important. The European supervisor will obviously need to oversee the national supervisors in a clear hierarchical structure and possibly have an examiner regularly present at the national supervisors. (A rotation system as in the US would not work well as it will give rise to coordination and informational problems (see Agarwal et al. 2012). Working closely with national authorities in an integrated system would avoid unnecessary centralisation of powers, duplication of structures, and the loss of knowledge on the local economies. As it stands currently, the Commission's proposal suggests that the ECB – the European institution put in charge of supervision – should "acquire competences" in carrying out the task and build up a new administrative structure for its fully centralised exercise.

But why the ECB? Why not?

As mentioned above, moving micro-prudential bank regulation and supervision at a European level does not necessarily imply moving it to the ECB. Why the ECB? As very succinctly put by Charles Wyplosz in a recent opinion piece borrowing from Bagehot (1873): every banking system needs a lender of last resort and a central bank is the only institution that can fulfill this role given the large amount of money that needs to be mobilised in a very short period of time, especially in the new interconnected world that we live in today (Wyplosz, 2012). For a central bank, however, to be able to act appropriately it must have intimate knowledge of the exact situation of the banks for which it is supposed to act as a lender of last resort in real time, which requires supervisory responsibilities. The underlying assumption here is that the channeling of accurate and unbiased information from other institutions that do not necessarily share the same incentives cannot be trusted, especially when there is no time or sufficient information to gather an own opinion. Under this argument the ECB – the Eurozone's ultimate central bank and lender of last resort – should have the responsibility of supervising the Eurozone's banks as it is ultimately responsible for maintaining the stability of the financial system and of the euro itself. As Wyplosz (2012) points out, this logic was deliberately ignored when the single currency was created, giving in to pressures from both banks and national supervisors. The Commissions's proposal essentially aims at correcting this 'birth defect'.

The lender of last resort argument does not apply to EU countries that are not in the Eurozone. These countries have their own currencies and their own central banks who can assume the responsibilities of the lender of last resort. In fact, the Commission's proposal does not transfer the supervision of non-Eurozone banks to the ECB, but allows them to join on a voluntary basis.[1] (Anything shorter than that, would have guaranteed that the EC's proposal will be vetoed by opposing countries.) As a result, some of the advantages of moving supervision to a European level – mentioned above – will fall short of reaching their full potential. For example, while the supervision of cross-border institutions will be on a consolidated basis for their Eurozone activities, there will still be need for co-ordination between euro and non-euro jurisdictions. Similar examples can be made for the other advantages mentioned above – although the problems with the uniform rules and their enforcement may be mitigated by the EBA's common 'rulebook' and 'handbook' that will apply to all EU countries, not just those in the Eurozone.

One important concern of hosting monetary policy and bank supervision under the same institution has to do with the potentially conflicting goals of the two tasks (see, for example, Goodhart and Schoenmaker 1992). Monetary policy is usually countercyclical, while the effects of regulation and supervision tend to be procyclical, offsetting to some extent the objectives of monetary policy. In particular, during periods of economic slowdown, the financial condition of banks deteriorates and supervisors step in and apply pressure on the institutions to improve their condition. However, the implementation of these requirements will typically result in tighter credit, reinforcing the recession.[2] Following this line of argument, one might expect that a central bank may 'go easier' on supervision to support monetary policy objectives. Supervision could also influence the conduct of monetary policy. It is often argued that interest rates may be kept lower than otherwise because of concerns about the banking sector, resulting in

---

1   This choice should be made at the country level (and not at the level of an institution). Opting in and out easily should not be possible, as this will induce strategic behavior and a 'race to the bottom'.

2   The slow recovery from the 1990 U.S. recession was attributed by many researchers to a dramatic decrease in the supply of bank loans caused by increased capital requirements and more stringent regulatory practices (Bernanke and Lown, 1991; Berger and Udell, 1994; Berger, Kashyap and Scalise, 1995; Hancock, Laing and Wilcox, 1995).

worse performance with respect to price stability.[3] Because of such conflicts, it is often argued that monetary policy and bank supervision should be kept separate, and when hosted under the same institution, 'Chinese walls' should be erected between the two functions. The EC's proposal seems to share these concerns as it proposes a segregation of activities between monetary policy and bank supervision within the ECB. Carmassi et al (2012) argue that separation seems hardly guaranteed under the proposed set-up as supervision will be under the "oversight and responsibility" of the ECB's governing council – they argue instead that setting-up of a separate and independent governing council within the ECB would be a better alternative.

Giving supervisory responsibilities to a central bank could also have some important positive effects. Peek et al. (1999) argued that information obtained from bank supervision could improve the accuracy of economic forecasting, and thus help the central bank to conduct monetary policy more effectively. Problems in the banking sector may serve as an early indicator of deteriorating macroeconomic conditions.[4] Using data from the US – where the Fed is responsible for monetary policy and the supervision of some of the largest US banks – the authors showed that supervisory information can and does help the Fed to conduct monetary policy more effectively. They found that confidential information on the health of the banking system (CAMEL ratings) is useful in predicting inflation and unemployment, but is not used by private forecasters or by the Fed itself in its forecasts. Although, the Fed does not seem to make systematic use of this information in its Greenbook forecasts, Peek et al. found that this confidential information is taken into account when setting monetary policy (i.e., it is found to affect the votes of the FOMC members). While they showed the FED's

---

3   During the 1980s and the beginning of the 1990s, the US interest rates were kept low because of the severe problems of the Savings and Loan Associations (Vittas, 1992). Central banks with supervisory responsibilities have been found to have worse track records in fighting inflation (Goodhart and Schoenmaker (1992). This is true even after controlling for central bank independence (see Di Noia and Di Giorgio, 1999).

4   To the extent that the 'lending channel' of monetary policy is operative, supervisory information could provide advance notice of changes in bank lending behavior (see, for example, Bernanke and Gertler, 1995; Hubbard, 1995; and Kashyap, Stein and Wilcox, 1993).

supervisory responsibilities affect its contact of monetary policy, Ioannidou (2005) showed that monetary policy also affects the Fed's behavior as a bank supervisor: when the Fed tightens monetary policy, it becomes less strict in bank supervision (i.e., an increase in interest rates or a decrease in reserves is associated with a lower probability of intervention). Monetary policy instead is not found to alter the behavior of the other two federal supervisors – the FDIC and OCC – who do not have monetary policy responsibilities. One possible explanation for these finding is that the Fed is less strict on supervision to compensate banks for the extra pressure it puts on them when it tightens monetary policy, either because it is concerned about possible adverse effects from bank failures on its reputation or because it is concerned about possible adverse effects on financial stability. After all the Fed is responsible for maintaining the stability of the financial system and it supervising of some of the largest banks in the US.

Although I do believe that combining the two functions under the same institution will result in cross-effects from one function to the other – existing evidence from the US that is reviewed above supports this belief – the discussion about conflicts of interests is a somewhat artificial. The 'conflicts' described above are genuine and are not likely to be eliminated by institutional rearrangements. Giving up one objective in favour of another will sometimes be unavoidable at the Society's level. Eliminating the problem at the level of a particular institution is not going to solve these conflicts. An important question is which institutional setup would resolve these conflicts in the most efficient way for the society at large. One could argue that internalising conflicting goals within a single institution may result in a more efficient resolution because of lower frictions in deciding and implementing policies and because of enhanced accountability. It may also allow the central bank to internalise and react to unintended consequences that monetary policy may have on banks risk-taking incentives (see Ioannidou et al. 2009 and Jiménez et al. 2009). On the other hand, supervisory failures, which to some extent are unavoidable, might undermine the ECB's reputation and credibility in preserving price stability (especially if banks view this integrated approach as access to a larger 'put option'). If a central bank is responsible for bank supervision and bank failures occur, the public perception of its credibility could be adversely affected (e.g., Bank of England and the failure of BCCI in 1991). It is therefore very important that the banking union is completed. Improving the end-game is of crucial importance for setting the right incentives *ex ante* and giving the ECB a chance (to succeed).

References

Agarwal, S, D Lucca, A Seru and F Trebi (2012) "Inconsistent Regulators: Evidence from Banking", working paper ssrn-id978548.

Bagehot, W (1873), *Lombard Street*, Kegan, Paul & Co., London

Berger, A N, A Kashyap and J M Scalise (1995), 'The Transformation of the U.S. Banking Industry: What a Long Strange Trip It's Been.' *Brookings Papers on Economic Activity* 2, 55-201.

Berger, A N and G F Udell (1994), 'Did Risk-Based Capital Requirements Allocate Bank Credit and Caused a 'Credit Crunch' in the United States?', *Journal of Money, Credit and Banking* 26, 585-628.

Bernanke, B S and M Gertler (1995), 'Inside the Black Box: The Credit Channel of Monetary Policy Transmission', *Journal of Economic Perspectives* 9, 27-48.

Bernanke, B S and C Lown (1991), 'The Credit Crunch', *Brookings Papers on Economic Activity* 2, 205-239.

Carmassi, J, C Di Noia and S Micossi (2012), 'Banking union: A federal model for the European Union with prompt corrective action', VoxEU.org.

European Commission (2012a), Council Regulation conferring specific tasks on the European Central Bank concerning policies relating to the prudential supervision of credit institutions.

European Commission (2012b), Regulation of the European Parliament and of the Council amending Regulation (EU) No 1093/2010 establishing a European Supervisory Authority (European Banking Authority) as regards its interaction with Council Regulation (EU) No.../... conferring specific tasks on the European Central Bank concerning policies relating to the prudential supervision of credit institutions.

Di Noia, C and G Di Giorgio (1999), 'Should Bank Supervision and Monetary Policy Tasks be Given to Different Agencies?', *International Finance* 2, 361-378.

Goodhart, C A E and D Schoenmaker (1992), 'Institutional Separation between Supervisory and Monetary Agencies', *Giornale degli Economisti e Annali di Economia* 9-12, 353-439.

Hancock, D L and J A Wilcox (1995), 'Bank Capital Shocks: Dynamic Effects on Securities, Loans and Capital', *Journal of Banking and Finance* 19, 661-677.

Hubbard, G R (1995), 'Is there a 'Credit Channel' for Monetary Policy?', *Federal Reserve Bank of St. Louis Review* May/June, 63-77.

Ioannidou, V (2005), 'Does Monetary Policy Affect the Central Bank's Role in Bank Supervision?', *Journal of Financial Intermediation*, pp. 58-85.

Ioannidou, V, S Ongena and J L Peydró (2009), 'Monetary Policy, Risk-Taking and Pricing: Evidence from a Quasi-Natural Experiment', European Banking Center Discussion Paper No. 2009-04S.

Jiménez, G, S Ongena, J L Peydró and J Saurina (2009), 'Hazardous Times for Monetary Policy: What do Twenty-Three Million Bank Loans Say about the Effects of Monetary Policy on Credit Risk-Taking?', Banco de Espana Working Paper No. 0833.

Kashyap, A K, J C Stein and D W Wilcox (1993), 'Monetary Policy and Credit Conditions: Evidence from the Composition of External Finance', *American Economic Review* 83, 78-98.

Ongena, S, A Popov and G Udel (forthcoming), 'When the Cat's Away the Mice Will Play': Does Regulation At Home Affect Bank Risk Taking Abroad?', *Journal of Financial Economics.*

Peek, J, E Rosengren and G Tootell (1999), 'Is Bank Supervision Central to Central Banking?', *Quarterly Journal of Economics* 114, 629-653.

Vittas, D (1992), *Thrift Regulation in the United Kingdom and the United States, a Historical Perspective.* Washington, World Bank.

Wyplosz, C (2012), 'On Banking Union, Speak the Truth', VoxEU.org.

About the author

Vasso Ioannidou is a Professor of Finance at Tilburg University and a research fellow and Board member at the European Banking Center (EBC). Her research interests include the transmission mechanism of monetary policy, bank-firm relationships, prudential bank regulation and supervision, and the interaction between market discipline, deposit insurance design, and moral hazard. Her work has been published in the *Journal of Finance*, the *Journal of Financial Economics*, the *Journal of Financial Intermediation*, and the *Journal of International Economics* and it has been presented in leading international conferences including the meetings of the American Economic and Finance Associations, the Financial Intermediation Research Society, and the NBER Summer Institute.

Banking union: Where we're going wrong

Dirk Schoenmaker
Duisenberg School of Finance and VU University Amsterdam

A piecemeal approach towards banking union is emerging, with banking supervision first and resolution and deposit insurance at some undefined later stage. This column argues that such an approach may lead to an unstable banking union and that any attempt at banking union must include an integrated deposit insurance and resolution authority in order to be successful.

The European Commission (2012) has presented its legislative proposal for banking union whose key element is a 'Single Supervisory Mechanism' to be headed by the ECB, but leaves resolution and deposit insurance at the national level. Is that viable? A recent paper by Pisani-Ferry and Wolff (2012) on the fiscal implications of a banking union argues that a common deposit insurance fund is not necessary at this point. The reason given is that deposit funds insure against the failure of a single, small financial institution, but not against the failure of the Eurozone financial system. They consider deposit insurance therefore as a second order issue. By contrast, in recent work with Daniel Gros (Gros and Schoenmaker 2012), I argue that depositor confidence can be strengthened immediately by a gradual phasing in of a credible European deposit insurance fund. Carmassi et al (2012) also argue for an integrated approach for the three functions of banking supervision, deposit insurance and resolution. Finally, Van Rompuy (Van Rompuy Report 2012) has presented his report *Towards a Genuine Economic and Monetary Union* with four building blocks. Building on the Single Rule Book, the first building block on an integrated financial framework includes European banking supervision, a European Deposit Insurance Scheme and a European Resolution Scheme.

This paper first explains why an integrated architecture for the proposed banking union is needed. The key element is to get the incentives right. Next, I argue for combining deposit insurance and resolution on efficiency grounds. The argument is that we need a few strong institutions at the European level instead of multiple agencies with partly overlapping mandates and information needs.

Architecture of a banking union

Economists use a 'backwards' approach when looking at the link between supervision and deposit insurance and resolution. The endgame of resolution and deposit insurance drives the incentives for *ex ante* supervision (Schoenmaker, forthcoming).

In the current setup, the EC is the rule maker and the ECB the lender of last resort for the European banking system. The EC is the key policymaker, initiating new policies and rules for the financial system. In parallel, the European Banking Authority (EBA) has a key role in drafting technical standards and developing a single rulebook for the EU internal market.

The new proposals for a banking union envisage a supervisory role for the ECB. In this article, I argue that there is also a need for a European Deposit Insurance and Resolution Authority (EDIRA). The final stage in the governance framework is the fiscal backstop. Crises affecting banks are commonly macroeconomic and general in nature, following asset market collapses and economic downturns. The existing national deposit insurance and resolution funds can thus quickly run out of funds (Spain, Ireland) and need the ultimate backup of government support. But a widespread asset market collapse coupled with an economic downturn can push even the sovereign into insolvency, as the cases of Ireland and Spain have shown. Then either the sovereign itself will need a backstop, or the backstop will have to come from a different source. The European Stability Mechanism (ESM) was created to provide the fiscal backstop for member countries, and possibly also the banking systems of member countries in financial distress. The stability of a banking system can be assured only if investors know that such a backstop exists. The arrow for the fiscal backstop is thus backwards in Figure 1, illustrating our backwards-solving approach towards governance. (See Schoenmaker, forthcoming, for a full analysis of a governance framework for international banking.)

Figure 1. European institutions for financial supervision and stability in a banking union

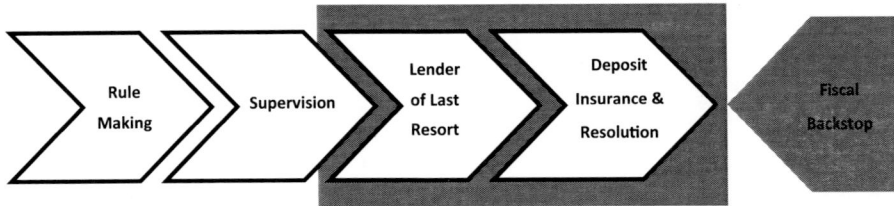

Note: The framework illustrates the five stages from rule making to the fiscal backstop. The bottom line shows the agency for each function.

Source: Schoenmaker (forthcoming)

A system under which the deposit insurance and resolution functions remain national while the supervision and lender of last resort functions move to the ECB would lead to serious problems. Dewatripont and Tirole (1994) stress the point that as depositors are guaranteed, they will no longer have an incentive to monitor the bank. Normally the supervisor then takes over the monitoring role representing the depositors. This is naturally the case at national level, where both the supervisor and the deposit insurance system are part of the same government. But this would not be the case for Europe if only supervision were centralised and national authorities remained responsible for deposit insurance and restructuring. The ECB would have an incentive to offload the fiscal cost of any problem to the national authorities.

As long as deposit insurance and resolution remained at the national level, serious conflicts would arise if the ECB thinks that any given bank needs to be restructured or closed down. The ECB would do this on the basis of its assessment of the viability of the bank and any danger it might represent to systemic stability at the Eurozone level. By contrast the national deposit insurance systems and, more generally, the national authority responsible for bank restructuring (i.e. in practice today's supervisors and finance ministries) would have a tendency to minimise their own costs by keeping the bank alive through support from the ECB. National authorities would naturally have a tendency to blame an 'unfair' ECB for not recognising the strength of 'their' bank which should not be closed, but saved. This type of conflict is likely to be especially prevalent at the start of the new system when the ECB has to discover all the 'skeletons in the closet' hidden thus far by national supervisors.

Over time other conflicts will arise; for example if the ECB has made a mistake and led a bank to take too much risk. National authorities would then have a point in complaining if they had to pay up for the cost of this mistake. The best way to avoid these potential conflicts and provide the new Eurozone supervisor with proper incentives is to move gradually deposit insurance and resolution to the Eurozone level as well, thus ensuring eventually the needed alignment of responsibilities. A gradual introduction would ensure that during the transition both national and EU level authorities have 'a skin in the game'. (See Schoenmaker and Gros 2012 on how to gradually introduce an EDIRA.)

In sum, a system of European supervision and national resolution is not 'incentive compatible'. A European underpinning of deposit insurance and resolution is an indispensable complement to moving supervision to the ECB.

Combine deposit insurance and resolution

Figure 1 depicts the bodies in the new European governance framework. While the EC, the ECB, and the ESM are existing institutions; the EDIRA would be a new institution. Although it is tempting to place the new resolution authority at the ECB, the functions of supervision and resolution should remain separate (ASC 2012). As supervisors have responsibility for the licensing and ongoing supervision of banks, they may be slow to recognise (and admit to) problems at these banks. Supervisors may fear that inducing liquidation before a bank becomes insolvent could, in some cases, cause panic in the market. A separate resolution authority can judge the situation with a fresh pair of eyes and take appropriate action with much needed detachment. The private banking sector also applies this principle of separation. When a bank loan becomes doubtful, responsibility is transferred from the loan officer to the department for 'special' credits to foster a 'tough' approach. Given the need for a fiscal backstop, the new EDIRA could operate in close cooperation with the ESM. It is nevertheless important to guard the independence of the resolution authority, as the ministries of finance govern the ESM.

Deposit insurance and resolution are in principle separate functions. In the US they have been combined. The Dodd-Frank Act assigns resolution powers for large banks to the Federal Deposit Insurance Corporation (FDIC), in addition to the existing FDIC powers for smaller banks. Similarly, the Deposit Insurance Corporation of Japan has resolution powers. By analogy, Allen et al (2011) suggest combining the two functions within some kind of European equivalent of the FDIC. The EU would then also get a deposit insurance fund with resolution powers. The combination allows for swift decision making. Moreover, the least cost principle (choosing between liquidation with deposit payoffs or public support) can then internally be applied in each case. That would also contribute to swift crisis management.

The EDIRA would be fed through regular risk-based deposit insurance premiums from the banks whose customers benefit from its protection, i.e. the European banks supervised by the ECB. Any new deposit insurance scheme has to face the problem of the transition to the new steady state (see Schoenmaker and Gros 2012). The establishment of a viable fund is important. A suggestion is to start off with a European deposit insurance fund funded by deposit insurance premiums. Once the fund is beyond a certain size, it can also be used for resolution turning it into a fully-fledged European deposit insurance and resolution fund. In that way, private-sector funds are available for resolution in crisis management. To ensure that sufficient private funds are built up, the cap on the size of the fund should not be too small (as is currently the case with some deposit insurance funds).

National deposit insurance funds have an implicit or explicit fiscal backstop of the national government. With the ESM up and running a fiscal backstop can be easily implemented for a Eurozone-based EDIRA. All one would need for an EU-wide system would be a burden sharing mechanism between the ESM and the other member countries (Goodhart and Schoenmaker 2009). In the case of the rescue package for Ireland in 2010, the euro-outs (UK, Denmark, and Sweden) joined in the burden sharing following the ECB capital key, as UK banks were exposed to Ireland and would therefore also benefit from enhanced financial stability in Ireland. That shows that burden sharing can be widened if needed.

Conclusion

The debate about banking union is running into the typical 'chicken and egg' problem: Most academic observers agree that deposit guarantee and resolution should be organised at the same level as supervision. But at present only the creation of a 'Single Supervisory Mechanism' (SSM) to be headed by the ECB is being discussed; with deposit insurance and resolution to be considered only later when this SSM has shown its effectiveness. I argue that the SSM is unlikely to work well unless an EDIRA is introduced gradually at the same time.

References

Advisory Scientific Committee (2012), "Forbearance, Resolution and Deposit Insurance", *Reports of the Advisory Scientific Committee*, 1.

Allen, F, T Beck, E Carletti, P Lane, D Schoenmaker, and W Wagner (2011), "Cross-Border Banking in Europe: Implications for Financial Stability and Macroeconomic Policies", CEPR Report, London.

Carmassi, J, C Di Noia, and S Micossi (2012), "Banking Union: A federal model for the European Union with prompt corrective action", CEPS Policy Brief, 282.

Dewatripont, M and J Tirole (1994), *Prudential Regulation of Banks*, Cambridge, Mass, MIT Press.

European Commission (2012), "A Roadmap towards a Banking Union", COM(2012) 510 final, Brussels.

Goodhart, C and D Schoenmaker (2009), "Fiscal Burden Sharing in Cross-Border Banking Crises", *International Journal of Central Banking*, 5:141-165.

Gros, D and D Schoenmaker (2012), "The Case for Euro Deposit Insurance", Duisenberg School of Finance Policy Brief, 19.

Pisani-Ferry, J and G Wolff (2012), "The Fiscal Implications of a Banking Union", Bruegel Policy Brief Issue, September.

Schoenmaker, D (forthcoming), *Governance of International Banking: The Financial Trilemma*, Oxford University Press.

Schoenmaker, D and D Gros (2012), "A European Deposit Insurance and Resolution Fund: An Update", Duisenberg School of Finance Policy Paper, 26 and CEPS Policy Brief, 283.

About the author

Dirk Schoenmaker is Dean of the Duisenberg School of Finance and Professor of Finance, Banking and Insurance at the VU University Amsterdam. He has published in the areas of central banking, financial supervision and stability, and European financial integration. He is co-author of the textbook *Financial Markets and Institutions: A European Perspective* published by Cambridge University Press.

Before his appointment at the Duisenberg school in 2009, he served at the Ministry of Finance and the Ministry of Economic Affairs in the Netherlands. He was a member of the European Banking Committee as well as the Financial Services Committee of the European Union. In the 1990s, he served at the Bank of England and was a Visiting Scholar at the IMF.

Funding arrangements and burden sharing in banking resolution

Charles Goodhart
London School of Economics

The Eurozone is moving towards a banking union. This column argues that if banking supervision is to be shifted to the European level, so too should resolution and recapitalisation. It outlines how the costs of resolving and recapitalising failing banks might best be handled.

Through the summer of 2012 there have been increasing calls for the adoption of a 'banking union' in the Eurozone. The single aspect of this that is now becoming clearer is that the supervision of all cross-border banks headquartered in the Eurozone and of all banks therein in receipt of officially financed capitalisation should come under the supervision of the ECB. Whether that supervisory oversight should extend to all banks headquartered in the Eurozone, and the relationships between the ECB supervisory staff (yet to be assembled) and the European Banking Authority (EBA), on the one hand, and the supervisory staffs in member states (often, but not in all cases, in national central banks), on the other hand, has yet to be decided. Meanwhile, the British and Swedish authorities are not prepared to cede or share supervisory control over their own banks to the ECB. Nor is this necessary for achieving the purposes of banking union within the Eurozone, so the latter will be the relevant regional framework.

One of the problems that a banking union might help to remedy is a tendency for national regulatory authorities to be too soft on or to be partially captured by their own national champion banks – institutions that often have strong political links and lobbying capacities. Another problem has been that such national champions, especially when cross-border, have become too large relative to the size of their domestic exchequer. If such banks should become insolvent, the cost of rescue can become so large as to endanger the fiscal solvency of the state (as in the cases of Iceland, Ireland, and Spain). One of the main purposes of a banking union is to loosen the links between national banks and nation states whereby weakness in the one can imperil the other. A third problem is that – as the experiences of Dexia, Fortis, and the Icelandic banks have shown us – sharing the loss burden of a cross-border international bank through *ex-post* negotiation has been fraught with difficulties.

If a banking union is to help in resolving such problems, the ECB must have the ability to close down the operations of a failing bank expeditiously. It must do so in a manner that does not place an excessive fiscal burden on the home state, while allocating any residual burden of loss arising from the failure of a cross-border bank in an agreed distribution amongst the participating countries. Banks do fail from time to time; even 'narrow banks', which are supposed to be perfectly safe, can fail (as a consequence of fraud for instance, or a loss from 'safe' assets). Good supervision should make failure less common, but cannot prevent it altogether. Since the supervisor is responsible to the polity, which has delegated its powers, the supervisor also has responsibility for trying to minimise, or at least to reduce, the externalities and costs of bank resolution in the event of failure. Thus if responsibility for bank supervision is to be shifted to the federal Eurozone level, by the same token the management (and financing) of failing bank resolution should also pass to the same federal, Eurozone level.

Of course, the hope is to shift the costs of bank failures from the taxpayer onto other shoulders, to the banks themselves, or to their creditors. But attempts to shift the burden, particularly in the midst of a general financial crisis, can lead to severe and unhappy consequences. The remaining banks will be too weak to support an additional impost, and placing the burden on a failing bank's creditors may have contagious consequences for other banks' funding costs and financing abilities.

So, at least in the short run, and in the middle of a crisis, there may be little or no alternative except to resort to the taxpayer to recapitalise, or otherwise to bear the burden, of resolving a failing bank (or indeed of a failing banking system).

Resort to the taxpayer?

Whereas there has been general agreement within the Eurozone to transfer supervisory powers to the ECB, there has as yet been no equivalent agreement on the concomitant issue of handling and financing bank resolution. It remains, for example, unresolved whether any recapitalisation of Spain's banks by the European Stability Mechanism (ESM) would ultimately remain the liability of the Spanish government (the ESM being eventually repaid by it), or would be shared out among the participating countries according to the key for the ESM's financing (which is the same formula as used for putting up capital for the ECB), or in line with some other formula. Thus, one other possibility that has been considered is that the home country should have responsibility for the eventual repayment of half of the cost of resolution/recapitalisation, and half remaining with the ESM or Eurozone resolution fund and financed according to the ECB formula.

With this in mind none of the above proposals touch on, or deal with, the cross-border aspects of a banking failure. What if a bank, headquartered in a small country, say Belgium, failed because of losses in a large subsidiary in another, larger, country, say France? That subsidiary would have come under the supervisory control of the ECB and of both the Belgian and French supervisory authorities. Is it then really to be the case that the burden for refinancing should fall only on Belgium and/or on the participating Eurozone countries according to the same overall formula, with no special burden on France?

Failures occur primarily because of losses incurred on bank assets (write-offs and non-performing-loans) rather than runs triggered by some random event, and the main perceived benefit of banks in each country comes from the extension of loans to its citizens. So, as Dirk Schoenmaker and I have already proposed, a sensible division of burden sharing would be to relate the relative cost to the distribution of assets on the bank's books at some time prior to the failure (see Goodhart and Schoenmaker 2009). There would need to be a large enough lead-time to prevent last minute rebooking of assets between countries. There would still be arguments. What if the bad assets were mostly concentrated in one country, while in another the bank held only safe, 'riskless' assets? Should it therefore be the distribution of total assets or of risk-weighted assets? However, *ex-post* renegotiations between sovereign states are rarely productive, or amicable (as evidenced in the cases of Dexia and Fortis). One does need an *ex ante* rule; and the locational distribution of bank assets seems to us as good as can be otherwise found. That said, there has been virtually no discussion, nor any progress yet on this front.

Resort to the banks

There is a widespread perception that the financial crisis was caused, in some large part, by bad behaviour by banks and bankers. Thus there is enthusiasm for making those same banks and bankers pay for the direct costs of resolving and recapitalising the banks. Moreover, this is seen as shifting the burden, relatively painlessly, onto the appropriate shoulders and away from taxpayers. Making the banks pay for banking resolution is an integral part of the Dodd-Frank Act proposals for resolution, and will almost certainly be the means of financing a resolution fund in the Eurozone, and possibly in the wider EU.

Requiring such funding from banks is not, however, without its costs to the wider economy. In so far as banks are thereby taxed, intermediation via banks becomes more expensive, thus meaning finance will become diverted into other channels, which may well be less efficient and just as liable to crises and breakdowns. Banks will pass on much of the tax, dependent on market structure, to other creditors in the guise of lower interest rates, higher charges and fewer services to depositors, and higher rates and charges to borrowers. In short, bank spreads between deposit and lending rates would rise.

Then there is the question of the mechanism whereby the tax might be levied. If the tax to refinance the cost of bank resolution were to be imposed *ex post* after the event to recoup the prior resolution expenditures, it would fall on the 'good guys' – those banks that were prudent enough to have avoided failure, at a time in the immediate aftermath of a crisis when they, and the whole system, would tend to be abnormally weak. While the tax could still be levied in proportion to risk characteristics, i.e. in relation to capital adequacy, liquidity or leverage, so as to influence behaviour and thus the likelihood of the next crisis, the fact that it would be imposed *ex post* (and so will have had no behavioural effect on the prior crisis) suggests that it would be levied pro rata on deposits, and/or short-dated liabilities. A perennial problem with the imposition of financial penalties (taxes) on banks is that there is no generally agreed definition of risk, so such imposts tend to be imposed pro rata.

If such imposts were to be imposed *ex ante*, in advance of a crisis, they could perhaps be more closely calibrated to penalise behaviour more likely to lead to calls to use such an insurance fund. They would then have a double purpose, both as a regulatory device to encourage good behaviour as well as a means of funding future needs for recapitalisation. Again, however, there are problems. The main one is that in setting the premia in advance one has little idea, apart from the historical record, of the likely future date or scale of the next crisis, and therefore of the size of premia that would be needed. A second argument is often made that any insurance leads to 'moral hazard'. Perhaps in particular that having contributed to such an *ex ante* fund any bank, however badly run or in whatever state, might feel that it would have a moral right to be recapitalised – and perhaps even have its shareholders bailed out –rather than be liquidated or taken into temporary public ownership.

Be that as it may, economists tend to argue for *ex ante* imposts, primarily for the chance of aligning bankers' incentives more closely with social welfare. Bankers, on the other hand, and their lawyers(?), usually prefer the *ex post* mechanism. Perhaps because arguments about the appropriate delineation of any such impost are then more clear-cut. As may be imagined, bankers normally win any such argument. Taxes on banks, levied in order to recoup past official expenditures on recapitalisation, therefore tend to be levied *ex post* along pro rata lines.

Resort to other bank creditors

Even if imposts on banks should be levied, so as ultimately to meet the costs of the resolution of failing bank(s), they cannot be used to defray the immediate up-front costs of recapitalisation or liquidation. For this purpose there is another current suggestion, which is to replace taxpayer funding by calls on (unsecured) bondholders, either in the form of conditional convertible (Coco) bonds, (which can either be in high trigger, 'going concern', or low trigger, 'gone concern', format, (depending on whether they transform into equity well before, or at the point when bankruptcy is reached)), or bail-inable unsecured bonds, of various levels of seniority. Low trigger Cocos and bail-inable bonds have several characteristics in common.

Moreover, bondholders have chosen to invest in the bank, and have presumably done 'due diligence', whereas the taxpayer will generally have no connection with the bank. The bondholder will often be a rich financial institution such as a hedge fund. There was anger in Ireland for example, when senior unsecured bondholders were repaid in full, leaving the burden on the taxpayers. But without specific legal priority for depositors or bail-inable terms on issue, senior unsecured bond-holders rank pari-passu with uninsured depositors. When Iceland repaid all Icelandic depositors, but not the senior unsecured bondholders, the latter sued. The case failed in the Icelandic courts (surprise, surprise), but has been appealed to the European Court of Justice, where as of August 2012, it remains to be decided.

If the Irish government had decided to make unsecured senior bondholders junior to uninsured depositors, and thereby impose losses on them, it would have led existing and potential bond-holders in other Eurozone countries to expect similar treatment. Such contagion would very likely have virtually closed off, or made much more expensive, an important long-maturity funding channel for banks in most other Eurozone countries. In view of the difficulties and high cost of such bank funding that was already in effect, the ECB is reputed to have placed great pressure on the Irish government *not* to penalise senior unsecured bank bondholders.

Imposing penalties on senior unsecured bondholders, but not on uninsured depositors, would have represented a change in relative legal status *ex post facto*. But giving all depositors (Cross-border? Foreign currency?) priority, and/or making a subset of bond or Coco holders bail-inable from the start, would be an *ex ante* way of shifting the burden of resolution. Even so it would, one expects, have adverse consequences for bank funding costs. If the expected alternative source of recapitalisation funding was expected to be the taxpayer, why would bank management want to issue higher cost bail-inable bonds? Probably the only way to get banks to issue them would be to make them a partial alternative to pure equity for regulatory, capital adequacy purposes.

Even then, when banks start to fail in a crisis, the costs of rolling over or issuing new bail-inable bonds would probably rise steeply. If banks either have to raise additional equity- type, debt at unpropitious times, or cut back on leverage and new loans, by raising spreads and toughening up on collateral, they will choose to do the latter, as now. Potential investors can walk away from bank equity and bail-inable bonds; taxpayers cannot opt out. The implication is that reliance on taxpayers in a crisis may well be a cheaper way of maintaining an existing banking system in place, rather than putting the squeeze on bank investors. But then maybe the public, and several commentators, see a case for encouraging a sharp reduction in the relative size of the banking/financial system.

While some of the investors in unsecured bank bonds will have been rich individuals and hedge funds, probably a considerably larger proportion will be held by pension funds and insurance companies. It is always the public who bear the burden of taxation one way or another. Taxation can, if so wanted, be made sufficiently progressive to make the burden fall on the shoulders of the rich, more so than imposing the costs on bail-inable bondholders. In some part the present enthusiasm for imposing the costs on bail-inable bondholders is a reflection of 'the grass is always greener on the other side' syndrome. When pension funds and pensioners get hit by losses in bail-inable bonds, the tone may change.

Ultimately the case for bail-inable bonds is that it introduces a market mechanism, in place of a government dirigiste control mechanism. And ultimately the case against is that this new market mechanism may prove considerably more expensive in a crisis.

When should a bank go into resolution?

Whatever the mechanism for resolving a bank, the sooner that is done, the less the likely burden that will have to be subsequently met.

Author's note: This paper first appeared in the October 2012 edition of the *Butterworths Journal of International Banking & Financial Law.*

References

Goodhart, Charles and Dirk Schoenmaker (2009), "Fiscal Burden Sharing in Cross-Border Banking Crises", International Journal of Central Banking.

About the author

Charles Goodhart was the Norman Sosnow Professor of Banking and Finance at the London School of Economics until 2002; he is now an Emeritus Professor in the Financial Markets Group there. Before joining the London School of Economics in 1985, he worked at the Bank of England for seventeen years as a monetary adviser, becoming a Chief Adviser in 1980. During 1986, Prof. Goodhart helped to found, with Prof. Mervyn King, the Financial Markets Group at London School of Economics, which began its operation at the start of 1987. In 1997, he was appointed one of the outside independent members of the Bank of England's new Monetary Policy Committee until May 2000. Earlier he had taught at Cambridge and London School of Economics. Besides numerous articles, he has written a couple of books on monetary history, and a graduate monetary textbook, *Money, Information and Uncertainty* (2nd Edition 1989); and has published two collections of papers on monetary policy, *Monetary Theory* *and Practice* (1984) and *The Central Bank and The Financial System* (1995); and an institutional study of *The Evolution of Central Banks,* revised and republised (MIT Press) in 1988.

The financial implications of a banking union

Franklin Allen, Elena Carletti and Andrew Gimber
University of Pennsylvania; European University Institute; European University
Institute

With calls for a banking union to resolve the issue of banking interdependence within the Eurozone, this paper explores the reasons behind such a policy, how it should be implemented and the possible ramifications.

The European Commission's recent proposals for a Eurozone banking union note that many banks have outgrown the ability of their home governments to rescue them, and emphasise the need to break the link between troubled banks and sovereign indebtedness.[1] A single supervisory mechanism (SSM) is proposed as a necessary precursor to the use of 'European backstops' (i.e. the European Stability Mechanism) to recapitalise banks directly. One way of interpreting these statements is that exposure to problem banks needs to be pooled at the European level, and that the only way to make this politically palatable is for bank supervision to be organised at the European level as well. Taxpayers in one country will naturally be reluctant to pay for failed banks in another if they believe that national supervisors are to blame.

However, the ultimate goal of the proposed banking union is said to be to ensure that taxpayer funds will never again be needed to support distressed banks.[2] Whatever

---

1   "Global financial integration and the EU single market have enabled the banking sector in some Member States to outgrow national GDP many times over, resulting in institutions which are "too-big-to-fail" and "too-big-to-save" under existing national arrangements." See here.
     "Many banks have developed cross-border activities and have outgrown their national markets." See here.

2   "To make sure that supervisory authorities have all the tools they need to deal with bank failures without taxpayers' money." See here.

     Michel Barnier: "It will be the role of the ECB to make sure that banks in the euro area stick to sound financial practices. Our ultimate aim is to stop using taxpayers' money to bail out banks" See here.

the merits of a banking union for Europe, it would be truly miraculous if it were to completely eliminate the need to use taxpayer funds (even temporarily) to deal with failing banks. For this reason, it is important that European leaders take the fiscal implications of the proposed banking union seriously.

Current Commission proposals for an SSM imply that transferring "ultimate responsibility for supervision of banks in the euro area" from national supervisors to the ECB will improve the effectiveness of such supervision.[3] Underlying this assumption is the accusation that national supervisors have engaged in regulatory forbearance of their perceived national champions: in order to avoid embarrassment, they are supposed to have delayed acknowledging problems and thus allowed them to worsen.[4] It is implied that the ECB will take a more hard-headed view of troubled banks and hence resolve them swiftly without fear or favour.

There is good reason to believe, however, that the ECB might in fact be inclined to treat failing banks (and particularly their creditors) more leniently than national supervisors in cases where contagion is a threat. Indeed, this risk of contagion is at the heart of the Commission's justifications for moving towards a banking union in Europe.[5] If the ECB perceives that imposing haircuts on creditors (or forcibly converting their debt claims into equity) might lead to contagion across banks in the Eurozone (an externality

---

3   See here.

4   "[S]upervision of banks remains to a large extent within national boundaries and thereby fails to keep up with integrated banking markets. Supervisory failings have, since the onset of the banking crisis, significantly eroded confidence in the EU banking sector and contributed to an aggravation of tensions in euro area sovereign debt markets." See here.

"The effective impact and implications of the single supervisory mechanism on the operational functioning of the EBA will be further examined in the forthcoming review on the functioning of the European Supervisory Authorities to be presented by the Commission by 2 January 2014. In that context, the Commission will in particular examine whether the role of the EBA with regard to stress testing exercises needs to be strengthened, to avoid making the authority too dependent on information and contributions by those authorities competent for assessing the effective resilience of the banking sector across the Union." See here.

5   "Given pooled monetary responsibilities in the euro area and closer financial integration, there are specific risks in the euro area in terms of cross-border spill-over effects in the event of bank crises." See here.

"[P]ooled monetary responsibilities have spurred close economic and financial integration and increased the possibility of cross-border spill-over effects in the event of bank crises, and to break the link between sovereign debt and bank debt and the vicious circle which has led to over €4,5 trillion of taxpayers money being used to rescue banks in the EU." See here.

that may not be taken into account by national supervisors), it may be more prone to bailouts than national supervisors. There is in fact a precedent for the view that the ECB might be more favourable to bank creditors than national supervisors; whereas the Irish government was keen to impose haircuts on bondholders in Anglo Irish Bank, the ECB insisted that they be repaid in full.[6]

The likelihood of the ECB being a more lenient supervisor than national authorities is compounded by the greater resources it has at its disposal. One implication of our recent work (Allen et al. 2012; Gimber 2012) is that authorities with deeper pockets face a more severe commitment problem, since there is no more credible anti-bailout commitment device than being simply unable to pay. Since the marginal cost of bank bailouts would be lower if the necessary tax increases or spending cuts were spread across a larger population, the ECB would likely have fewer qualms about raising additional bailout funds than national governments.

We do not wish to downplay the threat of contagion, with which the Commission is rightly concerned. The history of the Great Depression and the literature on the financial accelerator tell us that banking panics can have devastating consequences for the real economy. However, the Commission should acknowledge that its objective of preventing contagion may be in conflict with its stated desire to make creditors (rather than taxpayers) bear the costs of bank failures under a single resolution mechanism.[7] An important lesson of the recent financial crisis is that bank runs by depositors are not the only source of banking crises. When banks and other financial institutions are dependent on short-term funding, rollover runs by nervous creditors can cause their liquidity to dry up very rapidly. Perhaps for this reason, the authorities have so far been generally reluctant to impose losses on creditors. As such, it is imperative that future proposals for a single resolution authority explain how losses could be imposed on

---

6   See here.
7   Under the proposed single resolution mechanism, "In particular shareholders and creditors should bear the costs of resolution before any external funding is granted, and private sector solutions should be found instead of using taxpayers' money." See here.

creditors while avoiding systemic risk, or acknowledge that taxpayer funds may indeed be required to prevent contagion.

The proposals appear to suggest that funds for deposit insurance and resolution could be raised by levies on the banks themselves. The principle of trying to link the size of such charges to the riskiness of banks is a laudable one from the point of view of trying to limit moral hazard. However, given the size of Europe's banking sector, it is unlikely that adequate resources for deposit insurance and resolution could be raised without recourse to taxpayer funds. In order to ensure the credibility of deposit insurance and resolution arrangements, it is important that European leaders make clear where such additional funds would come from. Moreover, explicit provisions should be made to deal with the debts of Eurozone banks which are already in trouble.

Although a banking union with shared funding of deposit insurance and resolution could weaken the link between a country's banks and its sovereign debt, it is impossible (in the absence of an ironclad commitment against bailouts) to break this link at the European level. Furthermore, the collapse of a country's banking sector would still have a deleterious effect on its fiscal position even if taxpayer-funded recapitalisations could be completely eliminated. Reinhart and Rogoff (2009) find that rescuing the banking system often does not cost very much compared to the drop in tax revenues and increase in government expenditures resulting from recessions following banking crises. The broader effects of a recession due to a collapse in credit could potentially be ameliorated by a banking union if it encouraged cross-border lending.

In conclusion, we think it is unrealistic to expect governments to totally avoid providing funds for bailouts. The devastating effect of contagion and other types of systemic risk on the real economy mean that relying on creditors alone is not a desirable policy. Putting the ECB in charge allows the externalities across borders within the Eurozone to be taken into account and that is desirable. Hopefully externalities with other EU countries not in the Eurozone will also be taken fully into account. However, this has to be accompanied by clear and credible resolution procedures as well as burden sharing rules.

References

Allen, F, E Carletti, I Goldstein, and A Leonello (2012), "Government Guarantees and Financial Stability", mimeo, University of Pennsylvania and European University Institute.

Gimber, AR (2012), "Bank Resolution, Bailouts and the Time Consistency Problem", mimeo, European University Institute.

Reinhart, C, and K Rogoff (2009), *This Time is Different: Eight Centuries of Financial Folly*, Oxford and Princeton: Princeton University Press.

About the authors

Franklin Allen is the Nippon Life Professor of Finance and Professor of Economics at the Wharton School of the University of Pennsylvania. He has been on the faculty since 1980. He is currently Co-Director of the Wharton Financial Institutions Center. He was formerly Vice Dean and Director of Wharton Doctoral Programs, Executive Editor of the *Review of Financial Studies* and is currently Managing Editor of the *Review of Finance*. He is a past President of the American Finance Association, the Western Finance Association, the Society for Financial Studies, and the Financial Intermediation Research Society, and a Fellow of the Econometric Society. He received his doctorate from Oxford University. Dr. Allen's main areas of interest are corporate finance, asset pricing, financial innovation, comparative financial systems, and financial crises. He is a co-author with Richard Brealey and Stewart Myers of the eighth through tenth editions of the textbook *Principles of Corporate Finance*.

Elena Carletti is Professor of Economics at the European University Institute, where she holds a joint chair in the Economics Department and the Robert Schuman Centre for

Advanced Studies. She is also Research Fellow at CEPR, Extramural fellow at TILEC, Fellow at the Center for Financial Studies, at CESifo and at the Wharton Financial Institutions Center.

Her main areas of interest are financial intermediation, financial crises, financial regulation, corporate governance, industrial organisation and competition policy. She has published numerous articles in leading economic journals, and has recently co-edited books on *Liquidity and Crises, Life in the Euro zone with or without Sovereign Debt* and *Governance for the Eurozone – Integration or Disintegration?* She has worked as consultant for the OECD and the World Bank, and participates regularly in policy debates and roundtables at central banks and international organisations.

Andrew Gimber is a third-year doctoral researcher in the Economics Department at the European University Institute in Florence, Italy. His research interests are in banking and financial crises, macroeconomic coordination failures, unemployment and monetary economics. He holds a BA in History and Economics from the University of Oxford, an MSc in Economics with distinction from the University of Warwick and an MRes in Economics from the European University Institute. In the summer of 2007 he was a Research Fellow at the Institute of Economic Affairs in London, and in the summer of 2009 he worked as an economist at the Department for Transport.

How to design a banking union that limits systemic risk in the Eurozone

Wolf Wagner
Tilburg University

The Eurozone is attempting to resolve the problem of systemic risk within its ailing banking sector. This paper argues that while banking union within the Eurozone is a very real solution to this issue, it must be orchestrated correctly in order to succeed.

A key objective of bank regulation and supervision is to reduce *systemic risk*, that is, the risk that a large number of banks experience stress at the same time. In such situations, lending in the economy is likely to be impeded and a credit crunch may occur, leading to a recession and widespread defaults. Besides being costly, the resolution of systemic crises is also relatively burdensome. It is hence of paramount importance to have a financial structure in place that keeps the risk of systemic crises at bay.

A banking union has the potential to reduce systemic risk in the Eurozone. However, I argue that it also poses significant new challenges for the management of such risk. In this column I explain how they can be tackled. In particular, I identify four elements that a successful banking union would need to incorporate:

- A banking union should not just lead to a simple *pooling of risks*, such as by centralising national deposit insurance systems. This runs the risk of making systemic crises more likely. A two-tiered structure of national and European systems is desirable, ideally with an additional European backstop in the case of systemic events.

- When harmonising regulation, European supervisors should not fall into the danger of encouraging more similar financial systems across countries. In order to mitigate the risk of systemic crises, we need a *diversity of approaches* to financial intermediation in the Eurozone.

- A European supervisor has to avoid the build-up of *systemic imbalances*. For this a truly systemic perspective needs to be taken since even if individual countries are well balanced, the Eurozone as a whole may still have imbalances.

- A European supervisor should isolate banks from domestic pressure to pile up sovereign bonds. This can be done by introducing a cap on domestic bonds. Alternatively, diversification of sovereign risk can be forced through the introduction of synthetic Eurobonds or ESBies.

Let me be clear: the basic case for a European banking union is a strong one. A monetary union without a complementing banking union exacerbates systemic risk – as the current situation in the Eurozone painfully illustrates. Monetary unions are in particular not well equipped to deal with asymmetric shocks as regions cannot simply devalue in response to negative shocks. In addition, in a financially well integrated monetary union shocks tend to be exacerbated because agents can easily move capital to other regions, essentially leading to capital flight from the affected regions.[1] This worsens the positions of the banks in these regions. To make things worse, the potential of national governments to intervene is limited as the fate of banks and sovereigns is likely to be heavily intertwined in such situations.

A fully-fledged banking union has the ability to address these shortcomings:

- A European deposit insurance system reduces the risk of capital flight from affected regions and can thus stabilise the Eurozone.

- Banking resolution at the European level takes away responsibility from national supervisors who might be captured, or simply unable to recapitalise banks due to a lack of resources.

- Explicit rescue funds for banks break the vicious feedback loop between private (bank) debt and sovereign debt.[2]

---

1   While financial integration can help to deal with asymmetric productivity shocks, it may also amplify shocks to the banking system. See Kalemli-Ozcan and Papaioannou (2012).
2   This has been forcefully argued in a recent Vox column (Beck et al. 2012).

- A European lender of last resort (if part of the banking union) reduces the risk of self-fulfilling liquidity runs spreading across the Eurozone.

However, a banking union will also create new challenges for systemic risk.

A first problem is that any measure that solely pools national resources at the European level (through a European banking resolution fund or a European deposit insurance for example) can lead to an *increase* in systemic risk.[3] Consider a simple example of two banks, located in country A and B respectively. Suppose that a bank fails if the value of its assets, A_i (i=A,B), falls below its liabilities, D. Suppose that each country also has resources R_i to inject into its bank (either through bailouts or through the national deposit insurance fund). In the absence of a European banking union, the banking system of country A will hence fail if $A_A + R_A < D$. Likewise, country B's bank will fail if $A_B + R_B < D$. Eurozone-wide crises will hence occur if $A_A + R_A < D$ *and* $A_B + R_B < D$. Consider now a full pooling of resources, for example through the creation of a European-wide deposit insurance fund. This will fully eliminate isolated bank failures. Systemic crises will now occur when the joint resources of both countries fall short of the liabilities (when $A_A + R_A + A_B + R_B < 2D$). Such crises necessarily occur more often as now a shortfall at one country can also drag down the bank in the other country.[4]

What does this imply for the creation of a European banking union? For one, simply merging national deposit insurance systems is unlikely to be an optimal outcome. A preferred system is a two-tier approach with both national and European insurance in place. The national insurance system will be the first line of defence against domestic crises. The European fund (drawing from the national funds of other countries) will only intervene if the national fund is exhausted and when doing so does not undermine its ability to cope with problems in the other countries. Such a conditional insurance system can avoid the negative spillovers associated with a simple pooling – even if

---

3   See Shaffer (1994) or Wagner (2010).
4   With uniformly and independently distributed asset returns A_i, it is easy to see that the likelihood of systemic crises doubles.

no new funds are committed to the system. Note also that this system reduces moral hazard as in the majority of cases the costs will be borne domestically. However, such a scheme cannot effectively address systemic failures as the combined resources are not increased. If politically feasible, a European-fund should thus be equipped with additional resources to deal with systemic events.

A second challenge lies in the harmonisation of supervision and regulation that is likely to come about with a banking union. While such harmonisation is desirable from the viewpoint of eliminating regulatory arbitrage,[5] it also poses a great risk. As I have argued earlier (see Goodhart and Wagner 2012), a financial system that is resilient to systemic shocks needs *diversity*. If all institutions are subject to the same supervisory and regulatory environment, they will tend to undertake similar activities and react in similar ways. This enhances the risk of joint failures.[6] There is also no reason to believe that a supranational regulator is necessarily less prone to mistakes. (Just imagine if the excessive credit boom prior to the crisis were not constrained to a few countries in the Eurozone – but had taken place across the Eurozone as a whole!) It is hence of paramount importance that a European supervisor – while creating a level playing field – allows for a diversity of institutional structures and strategies. The supervisor should also ensure that there is competition among different approaches to financial intermediation (in particular, bank-focused financial systems should exist alongside market-based ones).

A third challenge is that of systemic imbalances. While a banking union allows for a more effective resolution of systemic crises, it should also be designed to avoid the build-up of systemic vulnerabilities and hence reduce (as much as possible) large scale crises from the outset. For this regulators need to monitor not only the exposures of individual member countries, but also the combined exposure of the Eurozone. For

---

5 Harmonisation, in addition, reduces competition among supervisors that can otherwise result in inefficiently lax regulation (Dell'Arricia and Marquez, 2006).
6 Even without homogenous regulation, banks are likely to undertake too similar activities. See, for example, Acharya (2012).

example, while each individual country may be well-diversified in its exposures, there may still be substantial risk if the majority of countries tend to diversify activities by specialising in the same region. As an example, the European Union was overexposed to the US prior to the crisis (which explains the strong contagion effect in the first phase of the crisis) even though most individual member states were fairly diversified (Schoenmaker and Wagner 2012). A focus on systemic risk also means that regulators can encourage diversity by allowing the banking systems of individual countries to have different exposures – as long as this does not create imbalances at the system level.

A final point is banks' exposures to sovereign risk. As many have noted, banks had over-accumulated governments bonds of their own countries prior to the crisis. This was a key factor in the amplification of the Eurozone crisis. If, for example, Greek banks had held a well-diversified portfolio of sovereign bonds, the spillover from Greece's sovereign debt problem to its banking system would have been limited. The problem of imbalanced sovereign exposures intensified during the crisis since banks used LTRO-financing and other rescue measures to increase exposure to their (troubled) sovereigns. This was either because banks underpriced the resulting risk[7] or because of pressure from national governments and central banks.

A European regulator can play a key role in limiting this risk factor. He can insulate banks from national sovereign risk by encouraging more diversification of sovereign exposures. This could be done through the introduction of a simple cap on domestic sovereign bonds. A more complete approach would be the introduction of synthetic Eurobonds,[8] which force effective diversification of sovereign bond holding in the Eurozone. Such bonds could be promoted by giving them lower risk weights in the calculation of capital requirements or by letting them become the collateral of first choice at the ECB.

---

7 Banks do not perceive the full cost of taking on additional sovereign risk since in the case of a failure of their sovereign they may fail anyway.
8 See Beck et al. 2011, and Brunnermeier et al. 2012 for a similar proposal.

Conclusions

In sum, a European banking union has the potential to reduce systemic risk at various margins. However, it also brings about its own challenges. The good news is that those can be largely avoided by a clever design of the institutions that underpin the banking union and by ensuring that regulation and supervision have a truly systemic focus.

References

Acharya, Viral V (2009), "A theory of systemic risk and design of prudential bank regulation", Journal of Financial Stability, 5:224-255.

Beck, T, D Gros and D Schoenmaker (2012), "Banking union instead of Eurobonds – disentangling sovereign and banking crises", VoxEU.org, 24 June.

Beck, T, H Uhlig and W Wagner (2011), "Insulating the financial sector from the European debt crisis: Eurobonds without public guarantees", VoXEU.org, 17 September.

Brunnermeier, Markus K, Luis Garicano, Philip R Lane, Marco Pagano, Ricardo Reis, Tano Santos, Stijn Van Nieuwerburgh, and Dimitri Vayanos (2011), "European Safe Bonds: ESBies", Euro-nomics.com.

Dell'Ariccia, Giovanni and Robert Marquez (2006), "Competition Among Regulators and Credit Market Integration", *Journal of Financial Economics*, 79: 401-30.

Goodhart, Charles and Wolf Wagner (2012), "Regulators should encourage more diversity in the financial system", VoxEU.org, 12 April.

Kalemli-Ozcan, Sebnem and Elias Papaioannou (2012), "Banking integration: Friend or foe?", VoxEU.org, 26 September.

Schoenmaker, Dirk and Wolf Wagner (2012), "Cross-Border Banking in Europe and Financial Stability", mimeo Duisenberg School of Finance.

Shaffer, Sherrill (1994), "Pooling intensifies joint failure risk", *Research in Financial Services*, 6:249-280.

Wagner, Wolf (2010), "Diversification at Financial Institutions and Systemic Crises", *Journal of Financial Intermediation,* 19:373-386.

About the author

Wolf Wagner is a Professor of Economics at the University of Tilburg. He is a member of the board of the European Banking Centre, a Senior Research Fellow at the Judge Business School at Cambridge University and a senior member of TILEC. His work has been published in various academic journals, such as the *Journal of Finance*, the *Review of Finance,* the J*ournal of Money, Credit, and Banking*, the J*ournal of International Economics* and the *Journal of Financial Intermediation.*

His work focuses on banking and financial markets. Since 2003 he has been working on issues related to the subprime crisis, such as incentive and risk-taking problems posed by financial innovations and the risks that arise when banks create opaque securities. Recent interests include the measurement of tail risks at banks, the impact of systemic liquidation risk on asset prices and the use of credit derivatives for risk management purposes.

US Banking over two centuries: Lessons for the Eurozone crisis

Joshua Aizenman
UCSC and NBER

As the debate over solutions to the European debt crisis drags on, this column argues that the Eurozone can stand to learn a lot from US's experience of debt mutualisation and deposit insurance.

The short history of the euro project has been remarkable. Earlier scepticism regarding the gains from forming the euro was deemed overblown during the 2000s. On the tenth anniversary of the ECB (2008), the euro's founding fathers brushed away the earlier critics, presuming that little can be gained by looking at historical lessons, as the euro project is unique and unprecedented.[1] However, the slowing down of the euro's periphery in 2010, at a time when Germany kept growing, awakened the market to the growing debt overhang of the Eurozone periphery, and to the incompleteness of the euro project. The resultant crisis is testing the viability of the single currency.

The Eurozone's recent history makes it clear that the tradeoffs facing the euro resemble the ones experienced by other unions throughout history. Thus, those who ignore lessons from history are bound to painfully reenact and learn them. This is probably because the formation of a new currency area is not unidirectional, and weak unions are bound to fail.[2] Evolutionary pressure purges arrangements and institutions that do not survive the realised shocks. Timely learning from mistakes may be the key for the dynamic viability of institutions, and the chances are that the US, Canada and other

---

1   Jonung and Drea (2010) exemplified the buoyant view regarding the Euro. "Never before have some of the world's largest economies surrendered their national currencies in favor of a common central bank. The euro is one of the most exciting experiments in monetary history." See also Weber's (2008) upbeat assessment of the first decade.
2   See Aizenman (2012) and Bordo and Jonug (1999).

unions morphed via a painful evolution into more robust institutions. While there is no reason for it to replicate the institutions of other unions, the Eurozone ignored their experiences at its own peril. This paper overviews possible lessons from the 19th and 20th century experiences of the US with a banking union, centralised supervision, and the logic of federal debt.

1.   States versus centralised deposit insurance

There are large gains from pooling risks from the states to the union level. These gains reflect both deeper diversification, and the greater credibility of backstopping the deposit insurance scheme at the union level. The Federal Deposit Insurance Cooperation (FDIC) in the US is the outcome of a costly learning process. Its birth in 1933-4 was the outcome of a political alliance generated during a deep crisis. Crises present opportunities for the creation of bold new institutions, when in the name of preserving the benefits of an existing system new institutions are needed to prevent the system's collapse. The initial blueprint of deposit insurance schemes and other regulatory institutions should go through periodic evaluations and changes, to accommodate the lessons of history.

The FDIC's formation and its 80-year history provide insights into the challenges of macro insurance and supervision. During 1829-1933, various US states experimented with state level schemes of deposit insurance with mixed success, and ultimate profound failure.

> "By the mid-1920s, all of the state insurance programs were in difficulty, and by the early 1930 none remained in operation. Consequently, 150 proposals for deposit insurance or guaranty were introduced into Congress between 1886 and 1933. The basic principles of the federal deposit insurance system were developed in these bills and in the experience of the various states that adopted insurance programs. These principles included financing the federal deposit insurance fund through assessments; the use of rigorous bank examination and supervision to limit the exposure of the fund; and other elements, such as standards for failed-bank

payoffs and liquidations, intended to minimise the economic disruptions caused by bank failures."[3]

Forming an institution like the FDIC is a major endeavour, as it needs the support of parties with diverging interests. Yet, no pain, no gain: deep crises provide opportunities for the formation of new coalitions which, with the proper leadership, may deliver more effective institutions. The written history of the FDIC states: "The adoption of nationwide deposit insurance in 1933 was made possible by the times, by the perseverance of the chairman of the House Committee on Banking and Currency, and by the fact that the legislation attracted support from two groups which formerly had divergent aims and interests – those who were determined to end destruction of circulating medium due to bank failures and those who sought to preserve the existing banking structure." (FDIC 1998, page 20.)

The short history of the FDIC reveals the need to change periodically the insurance risk premia, and supervision, responding to history and to anticipated challenges.[4] Crucially, the ultimate credibility of the FDIC rests on its ability to change the risk assessment to replenish losses, to engage in effective supervision and liquidation, and by its unique status, being backstopped by the federal government:

"The FDIC is funded by its member institutions through premiums and assessments paid on deposits. And, if ever needed, the FDIC can draw on a line of credit with the US Treasury. FDIC deposit insurance is backed by the full faith and credit of the United States government. This means that the resources of the United States government stand behind FDIC-insured depositors."

---

3   See FDIC (1998) page 18. In 1829, New York became the first state to adopt a bank-obligation insurance program. "During the next three decades five other states followed New York's lead. Except for Michigan's insurance plan, which failed after a short period of operation, these plans accomplished their purposes. Nevertheless, the last of these insurance programs went out of existence in 1866 when the great majority of state-chartered banks became national banks. Insurance of bank obligations was not attempted again by the states until the early 1900s. Eight states established deposit guaranty funds from 1908 to 1917. In contrast to the earlier state insurance systems, those adopted from 1908 to 1917 were generally unsuccessful."

4   The banking crisis of 1980s and 1990s had major implications on the functioning of the FDIC. Similarly, the 2008-9 crisis has propagated a new round of modifications.

2. State debt, debt mutualisation, and the stability of a currency union

There are large gains from limited debt mutualisation supported by a transparent dedicated source of taxation. Credible limited debt mutualisation serves to create a widely demanded safe asset, proving a cheap source of funding the legacy debt overhang. Limited debt mutualisation does not preclude the existence of a vibrant independent debt market for the union's states, restricted by each state's tax revenue.

The dollar is a 'successful' union of 50 states. Yet, this is the outcome of painful learning and a turbulent history of more than 200 years. A major challenge for the emerging federal government was dealing with the debt overhang after the American Revolutionary War (1775–1783). A brilliant resolution of these challenges was put forward by Alexander Hamilton, the Secretary of the Treasury from 1789 to 1795. Key elements of Hamilton's scheme included converting outstanding federal and state debt obligations into long-term bonds and creating credible mechanisms to service and amortise this debt. A sinking fund was created, setting aside in 1795 explicit revenues to be devoted to the fund: part of import duties, excise taxes on alcohol and other levies, and the sale of public lands.[5]

Yet, Hamilton's scheme did not deal with destabilising threats associated with future states' borrowing. In the following decades, states created and expanded their transportation infrastructure, investing heavily in their canals and railroads, relying deeply on debt funding during the economic boom of the decades that followed Hamilton's scheme. This boom came to an abrupt bust in the depression that began in 1839. By 1842, eight states were in default. In response, states' constitutions in the 1840s created procedures requiring state governments to raise taxes before they borrowed, and made those taxes irrevocable until the debt had been repaid. Wallis (2005) attributes the success and the stability of the US dollar union to these institutional changes: "After

---

5   See Perkins (1994) and Bordo and Vegh (2002).

the fiscal crisis of the early 1840s, states changed their constitutions to eliminate taxless finance in the future."

Are built-in fiscal restraints enough to ensure the stability of a union? Not necessarily. Von Hagen (1991) is skeptical about the effectiveness of fiscal restraints on states in the US: "Fiscal restraints significantly affect the probability of fiscal choices and performance, without however preventing extreme outcomes." An alternative perspective may combine the above views on the stability of a union. When the fiscal centre receives significant taxes from the states, and provides meaningful discretionary transfers to the states, the union's centre has plenty of bargaining clout. If a state misbehaves, the centre may cut the transfers to a degree that would prevent such behaviour.[6]

We close with reflections on the future of the Eurozone. History suggests large gains from buffering currency unions with a union-wide deposit insurance, and partial debt mutualisation. The credibility of a possible euro deposit insurance scheme requires a transparent funding and supervision mode, with a reliable backstopping mechanism. Establishing the credibility of such a scheme benefits from partial debt mutualisation and the formation of a dedicated Eurozone tax collection needed to serve these liabilities. Such a system may work in a lean federal system – deep enough to generate the necessary centralised funding, yet preserving considerable autonomy for the states. Building these capacities requires urgent investment in institutional modifications. A unique feature of the Eurozone is that, by virtue of its short history and its structure, the necessary modifications require contentious modifications at the EU level. While this process may be bumpy, the euro's future hinges on its success.

---

6   The centre's bargaining clout strengthens the fiscal restraints on states' over-borrowing. If this mechanism is powerful, the threat is enough to impose the necessary discipline. The states would refrain from running a large public debt-to-GDP ratio, and the threat of cutting transfers would be rarely used. In the US, this mechanism seems to be potent, as state governments receive a hefty share of their general revenue directly from the federal government – about 32% in 2009. Yet, if the credibility of the threat is questionable, it would be tested and used, as has been the case in Brazil (see Melo et al. 2010).

References and further reading

Aizenman, J (2012), "The Euro and the global crises: finding the balance between short term stabilization and forward looking reforms", NBER Working Paper # 18138.

Bordo, M D and L Jonug (1999), "The Future of EMU: What Does the History of Monetary Unions Tell Us?", NBER Working Paper No. 7365, published in Forrest Capie and Geoffrey Wood (eds), *Monetary Unions*, MacMillan, 2003.

Bordo M and C Vegh (2002) "What if Alexander Hamilton had been Argentinean? A comparison of the early monetary experiences of Argentina and the United States," *Journal of Monetary Economy*, 49, 3, pp. 459–494.

FDIC (1998) "A Brief History of Deposit Insurance in the United States".

Jonung L and O Drea (2010) "The euro: It can't happen. It's a bad idea. It won't last. US economists on the EMU, 1989 – 2002".

Melo M, C Pereria and S Souza (2010), "The political economy of fiscal reform in Brazil", IDB Working paper 117.

Perkins E J (1994) *American Public Finance and Financial Services, 1700–1815*, Ohio State University Press, Columbus, OH (1994).

Wallis J (2005), "Constitutions, Corporations, and Corruption: American States, 1842 to 1852", *Journal of Economic History*, 211-256.

Von Hagen J (1991), "A note on the empirical effectiveness of formal fiscal restraints", *Journal of Public Economics*, 44(2):199-210.

About the author

Joshua Aizenman joined the faculty at UCSC in 2001 following eleven years at Dartmouth College, where he served as the Champion Professor of International

Economics. He served as the Presidential Chair of Economics, UCSC, 2006-2009. His research covers a range of issues in the open economy. Joshua also serves as a Research Associate for the National Bureau of Economic Research. Other affiliations have included teaching and research positions at the University of Pennsylvania, the University of Chicago Graduate School of Business, and the Hebrew University in Jerusalem. Consulting relationships include the International Monetary Fund, the World Bank, the Inter-American Development Bank, and the Federal Reserve Bank of San Francisco.

The political economy of (eventual) banking union

Geoffrey R D Underhill
University of Amsterdam

As the debate regarding banking union in the Eurozone rolls on, this column tackles the subject from a different angle – outlining the political economy ramifications of such an undertaking.

The recent European Commission proposals for a banking union in the EU (Commission 2012; 2012a) stem from the need to take a range of short- and long-term measures to resolve the ongoing financial and sovereign debt crisis in the Eurozone, and to prevent as far as possible a reoccurrence in the future. The logic is the traditional European integration response of policy spillover *fuite en avant* that has often worked in the past: in a world of global market integration, the effectiveness of national policies and policy capacity are increasingly called into question, especially where cross-border capital mobility is concerned.

Open economies experience difficulty (sometimes severe) in maximising the benefits and minimising the costs of economic integration, and the pooling of sovereignty is one way to enhance state and societal capacity to manage these very real dilemmas of economic openness. Economic and Monetary Union and the Single European Market are highly developed institutional mechanisms that have proved historically effective at permitting member states to cope with a range of the policy dilemmas involved while retaining the capacity to develop a distinct national policy 'mix' that accommodates the often shifting preferences of national democratic processes. Just as purely national policy processes and institutions require consistent adaptation in the face of change, EMU and the single market as a policy framework were always incomplete in important respects. The crisis has exposed these weaknesses in dramatic fashion.

Member states therefore face a choice between the disintegration of the Eurozone and impairment of the single market, the two greatest achievements of the EU to date, or moving forward to fill in the relatively well-known institutional and policy lacunae in the governance of European financial and monetary space. Disintegration or indeed a failure to move forward would leave the most vulnerable states alone and saddled with the current worsening crisis and would pose significant risks, indeed uncertainties, for the global economy not to mention other EU/Eurozone members. Creditor countries would hardly escape unscathed. Indeed, there is considerable evidence that all along the principal beneficiaries of EMU have been the surplus countries such as Finland, Denmark, the Netherlands, Germany, and Austria (see Figure 1). In short, further institutionalisation of co-operation in the policy domain may indeed involve a further pooling and compromise of sovereignty (often eulogised in rather mythical and indeed Arcadian tones, as though sovereignty has always served humanity well)[1]. But further pooling will yield significant and indeed necessary gains for member states in terms of their capacity to deal with the consequences of integrated financial markets together with macroeconomic adjustment to internal and external imbalances. A range of solutions is possible, but choices must be made and political will and entrepreneurship is required.

This chapter will analyse the political economy aspects of banking union in the light of the recent Eurozone and Council commitments (Euro Area 2012) and the Commission's 'Road Map' (2012). Political economy typically focuses on a particular policy domain with a view to explaining a range of factors:

- The underlying conflicts of interest among social and political agents and/or constituencies (including of course states).
- The pattern of gains and losses to the same when change is either proposed or simply imposing itself.

---

[1] 'Sovereignty' in this context really means 'policy autonomy' as sovereignty is not in fact in question.

- The motivations and idea-sets behind the perceived preferences of the different actors and interests facing these changes.

Political economy also takes on issues of institutional and normative legitimacy in relation to both the challenges confronting political and economic communities, and the solutions that find their way on to the agenda. This involves examining the interface between the way in which 'economic' rivalries play out in a particular setting, how and by and for whom the rules of the game and terms of these rivalries and economic competition are set, and why in the face of pressures for change particular new outcomes result (or not). The setting in this case is the global financial crisis as transposed to the EU single market for financial services. This includes the peculiar arrangements adopted by Eurozone members to resolve sovereign debt problems, the overlapping institutions of governance at national and EU levels, and the increasingly volatile politics of protest and electoral competition. Given the gravity of the crisis, there are few who could not be considered stakeholders in this agonising series of events, yet unsurprisingly some are more influential than others at seeing that their preferences become institutionalised as rules of the game.

This column will argue that the battle lines over banking union is likely to mirror those of the creditor versus debtor members of the single currency to date. The various Eurozone members have adopted a self-interested policy 'discourse' that reflects their perceived preferences in terms of crisis resolution. These discourses unsurprisingly offer a poor explanation of the problem at hand, and thus deliver serially dysfunctional policy solutions. Attempts to implement a banking union will become a proxy for conflicts over resource transfer in the resolution of the sovereign debt crisis. So far the proposals focus mainly on issues of supervisory co-ordination and consistency, which is relatively uncontroversial. If the debate directly addresses the issue of distributional conflict, as eventually it must, progress is likely to be slow and solutions as far off as ever. Meanwhile the underlying legitimacy of the EU, and of its single currency, is draining rapidly away, potentially undermining the capacity of members to co-operate at all.

The doctrines of conflict

The solutions chosen by a particular political community (of which the EU and Eurozone are a loose if complex, multilevel variety) typically imply a particular analysis of the problem and an understanding that some ideas are better suited to solutions than others. It is important to point out that the analysis of the problem remains highly contested and that arguments on causality and responsibility are typically infused with a heady mix of enlightenment and solidarity (forward with more integration, we either pull together or hang together) in constant tension with self-interest (it was your fault so you should pay the most; we have the money so we determine the terms of settlement). It is difficult to disentangle the strands of enlightenment from those of self-interest. Even the perceived need for co-operation and deeper integration is of course fundamentally self-interested or no one would have had the idea in the first place, and neither the EU nor more global forms of governance would ever have emerged as they did.

One might separate out three stylised positions that each implies a particular direction for policy in the Eurozone. These positions are not entirely mutually incompatible and the actual positions of Eurozone members overlap these caricatures. Nonetheless, one may observe through caricature where most Eurozone members fit on whichever side of the divide.

1. Feckless spendthrifts: The countries that have emerged as victims of the sovereign debt crisis have for years spent too much and ignored their problems of competitiveness. The boom was the time for budget surpluses and implementing difficult reforms, and they failed, whereas we played by the rules and have been rewarded. These countries most likely should never have been admitted to the Eurozone. Some even misreported their debt loads and other entry criteria, demonstrating bad faith. Once they were in, they were little better at adhering to the rules. We can see that those that implemented a proper policy mix came out better. We are willing to help, but only if others take the opportunity to make the difficult choices and resolve their own problems that they created. If we take the easy way out via ECB intervention,

the opportunity for fundamental change will have been missed. A range of further integration measures strengthening monetary union is required, but these this will only work if member policies are subordinated to strict policy criteria, proper adjustment policies, and structural reforms.

2. Avanti integration: A monetary union among such a diverse set of economies was more of a political ambition than economic common sense. In view of optimum currency area theory, monetary union among such a diverse group of countries requires a much higher degree of labour market flexibility and a fiscal union ensuring resource transfers to deficit countries. Political union should have preceded or accompanied monetary union, but no one was ready for such a major step at the time. However, these deficiencies of monetary union can be corrected through a combination of above all domestic reform and, conditionally, further policy integration. Difficult choices need to be made by both debtor and creditor members of the union. Above all, the EU must restore confidence by demonstrating that the necessary fabric of governance will be developed and implemented.[2]

3. Out of the blue: Monetary union has been good for creditors and debtors alike, but particularly for surplus country exports. The Eurozone members most directly experiencing the sovereign debt crisis do have structural weaknesses and have committed policy sins. Yet this is nothing new, creditors are far from perfect, and in the run-up to EMU and following the introduction of the euro, much progress had been made by all. The financial crisis and ensuing recession was an external shock that no one fully predicted. The banking sectors of the crisis countries were not the source of the problem (with Ireland being an exception). Financial and property bubbles were widespread if manageable phenomena in good times. Surplus country banks did much of the dodgy lending anyway. The ongoing recession has ignited a fire that must be put out. We are willing to put in the effort to reform, but we need

---

2 One may note that discourse 2 is an 'outside-in' variant of discourse 1.

a rapid resolution to the crisis and to restore growth as societies can only take so much austerity.

None of these three 'policy discourses' properly explains either the problem at hand or the minimum conditions for either the successful operation of a currency union or the resolution of the crisis. Each overlaps somewhat with the truth. Creditor and deficit countries alike have sins of commission in policy terms. Those countries with relatively high debt loads had indeed improved the situation in the lead-up to and implementation of EMU. Some of the countries now in deepest trouble were among the best performers on debt loads and fiscal deficits (Spain, Ireland). At any rate, the debt problems such as they were had been known well before the crisis, as were Greek 'transparency problems' (well predicted by the IMF in 2009). Some of the countries patently not affected by the crisis have a rather heavy debt load, and Dutch or German banks were neither particularly well supervised nor unaffected by the financial turmoil – on the contrary! If anyone has a property bubble still to burst, it is the Netherlands. Not long ago, Germany was the country that had the apparently fatal combination of a current-account deficit and heavy fiscal deficits. Germany consistently broke and indeed altered the rules in its own favour. So government debt problems and property bubbles in themselves are unlikely to be the cause even if they are now the focus of the crisis. The pre-crisis policy stance probably has relatively little to do with the situation, though heavy debt loads are hardly likely to help in the resolution phase.

Not-so-prosaic realities

The financial crash is certainly the more likely trigger, because countries with greater or lesser structural and budgetary problems have been caught together. All countries have seen a worsening of their fiscal balance and debt loads as a result of the crisis. Bank rescues transferred billions of private debt to public-sector balance sheets, and the long recession has eaten away at tax revenues while welfare expenditures have risen along with unemployment. Recession and property market downturns (whether related to a genuine bubble or not) certainly worsened the situation of banks, even in countries not initially affected by the crisis, which includes most of those receiving bailouts or in line for the same. In the end, while a sound policy stance by domestic governments seems intuitively helpful, a good or bad policy stance does not properly determine whether a country is caught in the crisis or not.

A successful explanation as to what is going on needs to focus less on what states do and more on the patterns of cross border trade and capital flows under conditions of capital mobility and monetary union. Above all, the outcomes cannot be attributed uniquely to particular state players, though bad policy should make things worse. The outcome is above all a collective one fostered by the cross-border interaction of economic agents within the Eurozone and global economy. Capital market integration and capital flows are greatly accelerated by a monetary union where exchange rate risk is absent. The different EMU economies benefit from this in different ways, and run different sorts of risks. As one would expect, eliminating the risk of devaluation means that the benefits are certainly skewed towards the most competitive exporters – and under EMU their current-account surpluses have grown commensurately (see Figure 1). Meanwhile, the excess savings accumulated by the surplus countries flow through their banks to where returns are higher, often to the faster growing periphery with its well-known structural weaknesses. These economies gain cheaper capital and have fewer worries about the ongoing financing of their current account deficits (Jones 2003). Capital inflows spur growth but most likely also inflation, not to mention property booms driven by tourism and foreign investment. These effects potentially exacerbate competitiveness problems and may set up future bank problems in a downturn. In the boom, the situation looks positive and sustainable from both sides – a sign of investor confidence. In a downturn, however, the weaker economies fare worse because, well, they are weaker and less developed. The poorest regions of the weakest economies do the worst, which is no big surprise. This outcome is indeed inherent in the nature of a monetary union, as federal polities with domestic economies that are highly differentiated across regions know too well (Germany, with its five eastern provinces or 'Länder' from the former GDR, being a prime example).

Figure 1. From monetary union up to the outbreak of the crisis, the benefits of growing current-account surpluses of selected creditor countries reflect the deficits of debtor countries

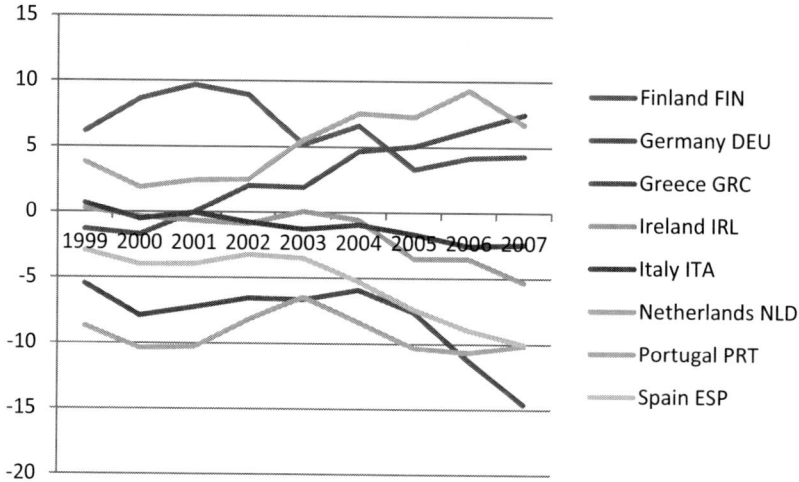

The institutional weaknesses and policy failures of the Eurozone have also been important factors in igniting the sovereign debt crisis. EMU was designed without a crisis management mechanism with each country looking after its own adjustment process even though the outcome was collectively generated. There would be no bailouts[3], and on the assumption that all would adhere to the rules, market discipline would ensure stability anyway (Underhill 2002). But following the rules of the Growth and Stability Pact would have been fatal in the financial crisis, so no one did (and some, including creditors, had long played fast and loose in the first place). Market forces, supposedly a discipline, had led in fact to imbalances and growing competitiveness problems during the good times. Then the crisis struck, followed by the costly rescue of the banks, recession, and more debt for governments. There was considerable ambiguity about what would happen if a country found itself in the rather broad margins between

---

3 Article 103, Treaty on European Community, http://eur-lex.europa.eu/LexUriServ/site/en/oj/2006/ce321/ ce32120061229en00010331.pdf

liquidity problems and insolvency. Would the no-bailout clause be respected no matter what? The former German finance minister Peer Steinbrück had once intimated: not necessarily. Would the ECB intervene as it had in rescuing the banks? Would defaults be an option? Would economies under severe adjustment pressures leave the euro and devalue?

As the crisis gathered pace around the problems of Greece in early 2010, there were no clear answers to these questions, but plenty of ambiguity and open dissent among Eurozone member countries. When the markets began to panic, there was a bailout for Greece that clearly made the country's predicament worse and the markets could see that. So bond spreads widened and the price of rescue grew geometrically as doubts over sovereign debt repayments worsened the predicament of the banks that held it, and vice versa. On the other hand, in a world of essentially zero and sometimes negative interest rates, the growing returns on distressed sovereign debt was a further transfer from debtor to creditor economies via the banks. The banks, at least it seemed, would consistently be bailed out by the ECB. The longer the agony went on, the less clear were the signals from the Eurozone governments, and those measures that were proposed were long-term solutions.

Debtor or creditor governments respectively settled on some variation of the three self-interested discourses above while promising underspecified reforms domestically and at the EU level. Market volatility and occasionally panic continued apace and debt loads grew alarmingly despite stupefying austerity measures. Domestic electorates lined up behind their respective governments, undermining what might have been popular support for further co-operation and institution-building. A monumental distributional conflict over the present and future of monetary union and macroeconomic adjustment had been ignited. Meanwhile, the benefits of EMU continued to accrue to surplus countries, but in lesser measure as economic growth began to falter and recession tightened its grip in the crisis countries. Contagion has made the problem immeasurably greater than if there had been prompt central intervention.

Banking union: political economy of doctrinal strife

So all three 'discourses' were actively employed both in a self-interested fashion and as a call to particular forms of further integration and solidarity. Furthermore, and crucially, banking union fits into all three causal/policy discourses but means different things to the respective proponents of these various policy stories. The proposal is so far the only major institutional innovation to emerge from the EU reform process following the financial crisis. Banking union contributes in particular to the goal of further integration aimed at restoring confidence in the single currency, and demonstrating that the EU is serious about further measures to ensure the successful governance of the euro. As such the banking union proposal may be thought to have a range of objectives, and therefore several potential gains for Eurozone and other EU member states in terms of policy capacity in the current turmoil:

- A consistent pattern of supervision, single rulebook, and single supervisor would improve the functioning of the single market for financial services.

- If properly applied, a banking union would further reduce opportunities for regulatory arbitrage inside the single market and better ensure uniform standards of compliance across the EU.

- A sound banking union would permit better supervision of systemically significant cross-border financial conglomerates, as well as more consistent enforcement.

- An EU-level supervisor should enhance the independence of financial supervision and reduce the potential for supervisory capture and policy clientelism in domestic financial systems, short-circuiting forbearance born of cosy relationships and economic interest.

- A banking union should permit better information-gathering for supervisory purposes and more comprehensive and uniform macroprudential oversight of the Eurozone and wider EU financial and monetary space to underpin financial stability

- A banking union provides for the mutualisation of risk and a further pooling of resources in a financial crisis, alleviating potential asymmetries among national economies when liquidity support is provided.

- A banking union should, through centralised management of banking crises, prevent the externalisation by national bank supervisors of the costs of national rescue and circumvent the blame game among national supervisors.

The proposal as it stands is far from definitive. In its current form, it covers these objectives to varying degrees. It is now up to the Council to decide on the balance that is desired. What should be clear from what has been argued so far is that:

- The various member states involved are likely to champion contrasting packages of these objectives as a function of their explanatory 'discourse' and perceived interests. There is no one member state in the council to speak for the interests of the Eurozone as a whole. The Council has overshadowed the Commission in the policy debate, and the ECB's mandate remains constrained on the issue of sovereign debt. It cannot behave as a 'normal' central bank would.

- Some aspects of the current proposals involve a relatively straightforward (if complex in practice) shifting of prudential supervisory responsibilities to the ECB. Others involve bank and crisis resolution issues that imply potential resource transfers. Although the current proposals insist that the new supervisory mechanism must "be combined with other steps such as a common system for deposit protection, and integrated crisis management (Commission 2012: 3, 6, 9-10)" with further draft legislation to follow, the current draft leaves these issues aside (Commission 2012a). The draft only deals with supervisory co-ordination and consistency issues. In this sense, the debate over banking union is likely to become a proxy fight about distributional issues along the lines of the three stylised explanatory 'stories' developed above. Already the German government has made it clear that a common deposit insurance scheme is off the table, and that the banking union will be permitted to address only the future of the system, not the current crisis or its legacy.[4]

- The quality of banking union as a solution will depend greatly on the quality of the analysis of the problem. To the extent that member states continue to cleave dog-matically to one or other of the stylised discourses discussed above and this limited vision becomes the core of the definitive proposals, then banking union may prove more part of the problem than a new and positive departure.

The starting point of banking union must be that in a monetary union, outcomes are collectively generated by economic agents through the interaction of creditor and debtor 'zones' of the union alike. The solution to the crisis had better be commensurately balanced in nature and focused on fact-based problem solving as opposed to the sort of doctrinal obscurantism that characterised the unfortunate Middle Ages and Reformation. It is clear that the balance of power in the Council lies behind 'discourse one' and a reluctant commitment to (a limited) 'discourse two'. This analysis will continue to yield solutions that are dysfunctional, worsening the crisis. Meanwhile, the countries that support discourse one continue to enjoy the skewed benefits of EMU.

There is also an ongoing failure to distinguish between long-run reforms, such as banking union, and the need for prompt crisis resolution. This is once again because prompt crisis resolution involves some form of 'federal' intervention, preferably from the ECB, in the same way that Canada or Germany stand behind the finances of their provinces.

Finally, a centrepiece of the G20 post-crisis proposals to reform policies aimed at financial stability was a commitment to a macroprudential approach to banking supervision. The current proposals do not refer to this issue at all, presumably because it too would involve questions of potential resource transfers. Banking union must surely give expression to the new, broader approach to financial supervision if it is to

---

4   See Financial Times 12 October 2012 among other sources.

accomplish its goals. Without a macroprudential take on the matter, one could hardly explain how the financial crisis became a sovereign debt crisis in the first place. So there is much missing in the current proposals, and an apparently low probability that the most important aspects of a banking union will be realised on anything like the timetable envisaged by the Commission and allegedly accepted by the member states.

The bottom line

There is one further, overarching element to the political economy of banking union in the EU. This concerns its political legitimacy and sustainability in the context of EMU. The serial collective policy failures since Greece first began to experience debt problems in late 2009 and corresponding failure to resolve the current crisis in a timely fashion have done little to enhance underlying support for the current form of either the EU or the single currency (or indeed open, liberal economies in general). Faced with cross-border market integration and capital mobility, the pooling of sovereignty is supposed to enhance national policy space and improve the effectiveness of national policies – albeit at a price in loss of autonomy in some domains and increasing policy interdependence with other countries. However, citizens in both creditor and debtor countries increasingly perceive rightly or wrongly that the common currency and perhaps European integration *tout court* have intensified economic risks and eviscerated the capacity of national political communities to shape their own societies and futures in accordance with domestic democratic priorities. Public opinion data and recent election results inform us that electorates are not unrealistic, but that support for further integration is increasingly contingent and indeed falling. Creditor country governments have not even bothered to make the case that the benefits of EMU, even net of bailouts, are skewed in their favour. They have instead drawn popular attention to the direct costs of bailout together with the alleged fecklessness of debtor economy governments and inhabitants. The failure to endorse the sorts of solutions applied in federal economies has only led to contagion, more debt, and the need for more bailouts. The EU and the

Eurozone in particular are caught in a downward legitimacy vortex. Without better real-world outcomes, this will only accelerate.

Banking union clearly cannot succeed or indeed proceed without adequate levels of electoral support, any more than the common currency can survive in such an absence. The central issues of costs, benefits, and 'who pays?' need to be confronted directly in conjunction with a viable and shared policy discourse that has a great deal more regard for the realities of monetary union than the doctrinal jousting that is going on at the moment. It cannot be the case that the citizen-taxpayer guarantors of European financial and monetary space can be expected to lend ongoing political support to the current institutional and policy mix while they take a long-run economic hit, especially the young; that their national policy space is permanently reduced and this becomes grounded irrevocably in national constitutions; that social risks can no longer successfully be pooled due to austerity – except perhaps in a few surplus countries (but for how long?). Are we serious, as the Treaty on European Union states, about "deepening the solidarity between [European] peoples", about promoting "economic and social progress" for the same, and fostering 'citizenship' in the context of "ever closer union among the peoples of Europe"? Or are we for a Europe of doctrinal smugness versus semi-permanent misery zones (in the long run we are all dead)? As I have written before, the Council and institutions of monetary union still appear more concerned with rescuing banks than citizens.

References

European Commission (2012), "Communication from the Commission to the European Parliament and the Council", COM(2012) 510 final, Brussels, 12 September.

European Commission (2012), "Proposal for a Council Regulation conferring specific tasks on the European Central Bank concerning policies relating to the prudential supervision of credit institutions", COM(2012) 511 final, Brussels, 12 September.

Euro Area Summit (2012), "Statement", Brussels, 29 June.

Jones, Erik (2003), "Liberalized Capital Markets, State Autonomy, and European Monetary Union", *European Journal of Political Research*, 42(2): 197-222.

International Monetary Fund (IMF 2009), "Greece: IMF Country Report for the 2009 Article IV Consultation", IMF Country Report 09/244, Washington D.C., IMF, 30 June.

Underhill, Geoffrey RD (2002), "Global Integration, EMU, and Monetary Governance in the European Union: the political economy of the 'stability culture'", in K Dyson (ed.), *European States and the Euro*, Oxford University Press.

About the author

Geoffrey R D Underhill is Professor of International Governance at the University of Amsterdam, a post he has held since 1998. He works on the political economy of governance in relation to international trade and the financial sector under conditions of cross-border market integration. He also has a long-running concern with theories of political economy, work which focuses on the relationship of patterns of market competition to shifting patterns of regulation and governance. His most recent work has focused on international co-operation for the regulation and supervision of global financial markets, the impact of regulatory change in financial markets on the global monetary system and the wider economic development process, and on problems of legitimacy and representation in global financial governance. He is author/editor of eleven books and over forty scholarly articles in peer-reviewed journals and edited collections. His most recent book, *Global Financial Integration Thirty Years On: from Reform to Crisis* (ed. with J Blom and D Mügge) was published by Cambridge University Press in 2010.